Free Roll

FREE ROLL

BRANDT TOBLER

Cover & Book Design by Nikki Ward, Morrison Alley Design

First Printing 2017

Lions Park Press

ISBN 978-0-9987948-1-5

NOTE:
I honestly believe that you own everything that has happened to you. Tell your stories!

If people wanted me to write warmly about them, they should've behaved better. Unfortunately my lawyers disagree. So even though all the stories in this book are true, I was encouraged to change a few names and details to protect the innocent, keep some cowards out of jail, and not let the world know that I may have had relations with a few women I technically wasn't supposed to. I was told changing these names would protect me from scumbag lawyers, the FBI, the IRS, Russian mobsters, Mexican cartel members, and psycho angry husbands. So if somebody tells you I am talking about them in this book, I probably am!

This book is dedicated to my amazing Grandparents Harl and Flora Petty. You never said it, but I know I was your favorite grandchild. I LOVE YOU!

Table of Contents

Introduction

This book was written by me, a stand–up comedian. It will take you through tragedy after tragedy on its path to the funny. Will it make you laugh? Eventually. Will it make you cry? Probably. But I hope it will also make you smile, dream and reflect, while simultaneously inspiring you to never stop chasing your dreams, even if your very own family is constantly trying to derail them.

Family issues, by the way? That's my story. I was raised on the blustery streets of Cheyenne, Wyoming. I couldn't wait to get out of the small town life to see if I could thrive in the big city. Before I knew it I was living in Las Vegas, carrying hundreds of thousands of dollars in cash, and risking my life every single day. I took a huge gamble on my life while literally gambling on behalf of some of the biggest professional gamblers on the planet. I found myself in a shady underground world of drugs, gambling, sex, and attempted murder. All this while trying to rebuild a father-son relationship that meant so much to me and so little to my "dad". My adventures have nearly gotten me killed on numerous occasions but, luckily for you, I survived long enough to write this book for your reading enjoyment.

I guess this book could be called a "memoir," but that sounds too fancy. I am far from fancy. I would rather call this book what it is: My "Collection of Chaos." And, as a three-time junior college drop-out, I am so proud for finishing it. I never thought I would write a book. Shit, I can barely write an email. But day after day I wrote. In crappy hotel rooms, smoky green rooms, and crowded coffee shops, I wrote. I interviewed countless family members and friends, asking them to go into great detail recounting memories they had been desperately trying to forget. I edited on seven-hour bus trips, proof-read on lousy airport wi-fi, and rewrote page after page while crammed in a middle seat in row twenty-seven between two nosy neighbors. And then one day it was finally done. Or at least I thought it was. (Cue another six months of work and editing!)

The process of writing this book has been a lot like my life. Things haven't always come easy, but I tried to keep going, every single day. I hope this book will inspire you to do the same, whether you dream of being on the comedic stage yourself or following some other wild adventure of your own making.

Brandt Tobler

Defined.

The exact definition of a free roll is not one you will find in a dictionary. It is a term I learned from Keith, my boss and mentor, the first day I started working for him as a professional gambler. My job entailed running up and down the Las Vegas strip betting hundreds of thousands of dollars each day while trying not to get robbed or killed. On my first day of work I heard him say it three or four times and I had never heard the term, so I asked him what it meant. He explained it like this; "There are two different kinds of free rolls: there's your traditional free roll and then there's every gambler's enemy, the free roll for disaster."

The easiest way to explain a free roll is this: Imagine that I give you two dice and say you get one roll. If you get a seven I will give you a million dollars, but if you roll any number beside a seven you get nothing. That means you have a 16.7% shot at a million dollars, and an 83.3% chance of gaining nothing, but also losing nothing. Essentially, you have a free shot at $1,000,000. Sure, it's only a 16.7% chance at a cool million, but only a positive outcome can come of it – it's a free roll. Now a free roll for disaster is fundamentally the same thing, but this time the result can only be negative.

Imagine that I give you two dice again. This time if you roll a seven I get your house and car, but if you roll anything else you lose nothing, and you gain nothing. Essentially, you have a free shot at losing your house and car. Now that 16.7% number feels a whole lot more likely and the thought of losing your home and your car feels far more real. This is an example of a free roll for disaster. He always said, "The key to life is to find opportunities to free roll as often as you can, and try to limit the free rolls for disaster."

Here is a perfect real life example: If somebody bought this book for you, you are now on a free roll. This book cost you nothing, and you now have a free shot at reading a great book (I know you will enjoy it). If you have awful taste and by the second page you hate it, you can give it to somebody else and you will have lost nothing. (If you are the original buyer, THANK YOU). An example of a free roll for disaster would be if you bought this book and you love it, but then an annoying acquaintance named Mark asks to borrow it. You can't stand Mark, and you have no idea why your friend Ashley keeps bringing him to your

house. But, because you are a very generous person, you reluctantly loan it to him. Now only two things can happen and they are both bad. Mark could take the book and never return it; now you've lost your favorite book. Even worse, he does return it; now that annoying guy Mark will be in your house again. Both outcomes are no good. That's a free roll for disaster. Now that you know how a free roll works, I think you will be shocked to notice how many times you find yourself on a free roll in your everyday life. And hopefully you can limit the number of occasions you are free rolling for disaster. (P.S. Don't let Mark borrow this book. He sucks.)

*H*e was a lying, cheating, manipulative, abusive, drug-addicted thief, but everybody said I had to love him because he was my dad. But then I found myself hugging and consoling my little brother as he laid crying uncontrollably on the floor and I only had one thought in my head: enough is enough. He had hurt everybody in my family both emotionally and physically his whole life. But this would be the last time he made anybody I love cry. I would end the pain once and for all. I would kill my dad. (More on that later.)

But let's start at the beginning. David Tobler, the paterfamilias, was a three-sport athlete. He played football, basketball, and ran track. He was considered one of the best athletes in the region. He hailed from Dix, Nebraska, a quarter-square mile town nestled in the southwest corner of the Nebraska panhandle. Most of Dix's two-hundred and twenty-five residents make their living on farms that were handed down from generation to generation. They take pride in working hard in wheat fields and raising cattle. My dad wasn't like most of the residents. After graduating high school in 1973, Dad went to a small college in northern Nebraska with the goal of playing college athletics and

getting a degree in physical education. His first semester away from home was spent drinking nightly and rarely going to class. He quickly realized that college was not for him and dropped out of school. Dad decided to follow my grandfather Duane and his older brother (my uncle Dennis) seventy miles due west from Dix, across the state line, to Cheyenne, Wyoming. The three of them found work on the Union Pacific Railroad. Duane had been making the daily commute to Cheyenne for almost a decade. He would rush home after work each night to spend time with his wife and four kids. The railroad was a good old boys club run mostly on seniority, and everybody took care of one another. Once hired, it was almost impossible to lose one's job.

The Tobler boys loved working for the railroad, mainly because it was a fairly easy job where they spent most days just riding on a train. They made close to $45,000 a year, one of the highest-paid jobs in the state. After work each day, Dad, Grandpa, and Uncle Dennis loved to frequent the Green Door, a strip club located two blocks from the depot. They would drink whiskey and promise young strippers that they could change their lives. Today the Green Door is the dirtiest dive of a strip club I've been too yet—and that's saying a lot considering where I've lived. (To give you some idea: There is no DJ, so the girls have to select their own songs on the jukebox. The stage is no bigger than a picnic table and there is no pole on the stage, only a small metal bar hanging from the ceiling that I would make a large bet could hold a rhino.) My dad, uncle, and grandpa loved this club because the owner would usually bus in new, beautiful dancers from Denver and Salt Lake City each week.

On one bitter-cold and snowy winter night, my dad was frustrated that the strip club didn't bring in new dancers that week, so he and his friends decided to stumble down the block to the Redwood bar. It was just his luck that a cute young lady named Kim would be there too. She was having a girls night out with her best friend and little sister. She noticed my dad the second she walked into the bar where he and his buddies were playing pool. In small towns like Cheyenne everybody tends to know each other, so my mom was shocked when she saw this tall handsome man she had never seen before. She immediately got a couple of quarters from the bartender, walked over, and set the quarters on the edge of the pool table. This got their attention. And as they all stared at her she sheepishly asked, "Can I play the winner?" My dad gave her a big grin. He looked at his current pool partner and said, "You just lost," and began to rack the balls to start the next game. He walked around the corner of the table and introduced himself to my mom.

"Hello beautiful, my name is David. It's so nice to meet you."

For the next two hours he laid the charm on my mom, paying for her and her friends' drinks all night long. My mom was very impressed with him. Not only was he good looking; he was funny. She really enjoyed talking to him. But there was one big problem… my mom was engaged.

Earlier in the year her high school sweetheart Tom, whom she had met when she was fifteen and been dating the last seven years, decided to pop the question. The wedding was only a couple months away and this night was what she considered one of her last chances to go out with just the girls. She had no intention of even talking to guys that night; she just wanted to have fun and dance. But as the evening went on and she continued having fun with my dad, it hit her like a ton of bricks: this wedding was a mistake.

She loved Tom, but he was like a buddy. Not somebody she wanted to spend the rest of her life with. At the end of the night, my mom thanked my dad and slipped him her phone number before she walked out to her car. My dad called my mom the very next day and they met up for dinner and drinks. After that night, they began sneaking around and seeing each other almost every day for the next month. Everybody in town knew my mom was engaged, so they had to be careful. Most nights they'd hide out at her best friend Candy's house. After a while, my mom was confident that her fiancé knew something was going on, so she decided she had to call off the wedding.

The wedding date was still two months away. She figured that was more than enough time to cancel everything her mom had set up. Well, when my grandma heard this, she disagreed. When my mom told her that she was going to cancel the wedding, my grandmother said, "The hell you are! I have already paid for the church, the reception, and we have two-hundred-and-fifty guests coming. YOU WILL GET MARRIED!" That night she told my dad what my grandma said, and he was not happy. He said, "I don't care what your mom said. I have a better plan." He decided that on the day of the wedding he would park down the street in his brand new white convertible Cadillac, and when my mom got a chance she would sneak out the back door of the church and hop into his car. They would then make the eighty-five-mile drive east to my dad's grandmother's house in central Nebraska, where nobody would find them. My mom knew that this was going to upset all of her friends and family, but more than that she knew she didn't want to marry Tom, so she told my dad, "Let's do it!"

Over the next couple days, my mom and dad went to the church several times to plan the best escape route for the runaway bride. They figured out which door she would exit, where he would park, and they did practice runs to see how long it would take her to get to the car. She introduced my dad to the people in the church as her cousin the wedding photographer, and the church let them have free-reign of the building to set up their plan. My mom later told me that planning her escape was more fun than planning the actual wedding.

The morning of the wedding my mom rode to the church with her mom and sister and put on her best fake smile. She told everybody that she was so excited for her big day. They got to the church three hours early and she and her bridesmaids were all in a back room drinking champagne and getting ready. She hadn't told anyone her plan, and as the time was getting closer she was getting more and more nervous. She knew if she went through with this everybody would hate her. But she also knew it's what she had to do. My dad told her he would be parked and waiting in the back of the church at 2:30 PM. That was a half-hour before the wedding, and would be the perfect time to tell her bridesmaids she needed a minute alone. As soon as everybody left the room, she would tiptoe out the back door, and be in my dad's car in thirty-three seconds.

At 2:25 PM she asked everybody to leave the room so she could gather her thoughts. My concerned Grandma asked if she wanted her to stay

"No mom, I just need a couple minutes to myself."

Before my grandmother walked out, she gave Mom a big hug and whispered, "Kim you look so beautiful today. I am so proud of you. Today will be the best day of your life."

This was the last thing my mom wanted to hear in that moment. She loved her mom more than anything in the world, and knew this would crush her. My mom sat there alone, looking back and forth at the clock and the back door. She knew if she went out that door it would change her life forever. At 2:29 PM she took a deep breath, stood up, and walked to the back door. She slowly cracked the back door and peeked out to make sure nobody watching. She then looked to the right to make sure my dad was parked and ready. She was ready to go! Unfortunately for her, my dad was not. His car wasn't where it was supposed to be and he was nowhere to be found. My mom closed the door and began to cry as she sat back down.

The second she sat down there was a knock on the door. She said, "Come in," thinking maybe it was my dad. But it was only the pastor coming in to check on her. He saw her crying and reassured her that everything was going to be okay. The Lord would take care of her and Tom, and they would have an amazing life together. She smiled. "I know pastor, I am just really scared." And she was scared. Only she knew she was in love with another man, a man she was willing to throw everything away for; a man who had forgotten to pick her up.

She touched up her makeup, chugged a glass of champagne, put an enormous fake smile on her face, and told her mom and bridesmaids, "Let's go get me married!" She went along with the wedding that afternoon and it was a complete disaster. Tom had celebrated his bachelor party the night before, and his dumb-ass friends had gotten him high on horse tranquilizers. He struggled to walk down the aisle and mumbled through his vows because he could barely talk.

The pastor pronounced them husband and wife, and my mom said his breath reeked of alcohol during their first, awful, official kiss. As they walked out of the massive church doors and down the steps, she kept the fake smile on while everybody took pictures and threw rice at the newly-married couple. When my mom got to the bottom of the stairs she looked to her left, and about a block away she saw my dad sitting in his Cadillac, watching everybody file out of the church. Tom and his idiot friends had ridden their motorcycles to the wedding, and my mom was not going to get on the back of his bike in her beautiful long white dress. She told Tom she was going to ride to the reception with her bridesmaids. On the way to the reception, my mom told Candy to drive by the Four Winds Bar. Candy began to ask questions, confused as to why they were heading to a bar and not the reception. She told my mom, "If you want to hit a bar for a quick drink, let's stop at one that's on the way." My mom was persistent. "It's my wedding day, take me to the fucking Four Winds now!" She wanted an explanation and she knew that's where my dad would be.

My mom walked into the bar, in her wedding dress, and found my dad sitting in his usual spot. "What the hell happened? Where were you at two-thirty?"

He was already drunk. He was called in to work the next day so he wouldn't be able to leave town with her. If he missed another day of work, he would be in big trouble with his boss. My mom was furious. She was about to upset everybody in her life, and he was worried about getting written up at work? My mom stomped out of the bar and went to her wedding reception. When she got to the country club, she was ready to enjoy a night of drinking and dancing with her family and friends, but that never happened. She spent the whole night babysitting her new, drunk husband. By the end of the evening, the sight of him made her sick.

The next morning the newlyweds had a flight to San Diego for their honeymoon. If you have ever been to San Diego, you know it is a very hard place to hate, but my mom hated every second of it. She didn't want to be with Tom and spent every waking moment of the trip thinking about my dad. She was still mad at him for not sticking with their wedding day plan, but she missed all the fun they had when they were together. She wanted to leave Tom, but now she felt trapped. When they returned home from their honeymoon there was a brand new car waiting for my mom. She said Tom felt guilty about being such a mess on their wedding day. Tom had also bought them a house two weeks before the wedding. Despite her feelings for Tom, my mom was thrilled about her new car and the beautiful house he had bought for her. Maybe, she hoped, things would get better. But as they moved in, she quickly started to hate the way he treated her in their new home. Tom was very territorial of "his" house. She was not allowed to hang pictures or pick out any furniture. This new house didn't feel like a loving home at all. After trying to be a good wife for the first three weeks, she made the decision that she couldn't do it anymore.

She wanted to see my dad. And he would be easy to find, considering he went to the same two bars every day. They soon reconnected and began hanging out every day, and this time my mom didn't even try to sneak around. She never wanted to be married in the first place, and she refused to go on with this charade.

She started spending every day at my dad's shitty trailer and would come home at all hours of the night. Tom knew something was going on, but whenever he would confront my mom she would lie and say she was at Candy's house. After a while, Tom started driving by Candy's house nightly and, of course, he never saw the new car he bought my mom. He finally decided enough was enough and confronted Candy. Candy, being the amazing best friend that she was, told Tom all about David and actually drove Tom to my dad's trailer.

When they got to the trailer, Tom got out of the car and knocked on the front door. He knocked and then pounded, but nobody answered. My mom and dad had been drinking and getting high all night, and had passed out in his bed. In his frustration, Tom walked around the trailer, peeking in the windows. When he got to my dad's bedroom, he found the window right above the bed and looked in. They were right below him, fast asleep. In a jealous rage, he punched the window with his right hand, shattering glass all over the bed. As pieces of glass scattered onto my mom's face, she woke up in a panic.

She looked up to see her husband's face about a foot away from her. Tom was screaming at her and climbing through the broken window. He proceeded to flop down onto my startled parents. My dad was still drunk and disoriented as Tom's bloody right hand punched him in the nose. The blood gushing into his mouth sobered him up quickly. He hopped out of bed and was ready for a fight to the death in just his tighty-whities and tube socks. My mom jumped between the two of them and tried to keep them separated. She pushed Tom out the front door while my dad struggled to get dressed. Once my dad got his pants and boots on, he ran outside, ready to fight in his front yard. By this time my mom and Candy had managed to get Tom back into Candy's car and he was screaming out the passenger window as Candy sped away. He was calling my mom a whore and promising that he would beat my dad's ass the next time he saw him.

My mom was scared to go home and face her husband. She knew she needed to apologize to Tom and tell him the truth: that she didn't want to be with him. She went back inside to grab her keys and purse, and gave my dad a big kiss on her way out the front door. When she got to her car, she realized there was another problem. She must have forgotten to put out her cigarette when she got to the trailer, and now the interior of the brand new car was burnt to a crisp. She called Tom and told him she wanted to come home and talk about everything, but she couldn't, because the interior of her car was ruined. She explained what had happened and asked if he would pick her and the car up. Hearing this, Tom was immediately convinced that my dad had done it, and launched into a tirade about how he and his gang of biker friends were going to kill him.

About an hour later, Tom showed up with three friends. They towed the car and took my mom home. My mom made my dad promise he would stay inside when Tom arrived so there would be no more drama. My father agreed, but told her that Tom would need to pay for the window he had broken. I find this moment in the story to be particularly hilarious considering that my dad broke up Tom's marriage. If you ask me, they both kind of wrecked each other's home/trailer.

When my mom and Tom got back to their house, my mom told him lie after lie, totally scrapping her original plan of telling him she wanted a divorce. Tom was not the smartest guy and really loved my mom, so she could usually get him to believe anything. My mom told him that she and David were just friends and that nothing sexual has ever happened between them. She said that they had just gotten way too drunk and passed out. She told Tom that my dad really liked Candy and that she had gone over there to talk to him about her. I can't imagine how Tom could have possibly believed that bullshit story, but he did. He said he would forgive her if she promised to never see him again. My mom made that promise, knowing that she was going to call my dad the second Tom left the house.

And that's exactly what she did.

My dad and his railroad buddies had been planning a camping trip for the upcoming weekend, and my mom had been looking forward to it from the moment she was invited. That Friday morning, as Tom was pulling out of the driveway to go to work, my mom was on the phone letting my dad know she was ready to be picked up and head out to the lake. My mom said those next three days at the lake were one of the best weekends of her life. The weather was beautiful and the company was great. They spent all day on the boat drinking and partying, and all night cuddled up laughing by the campfire. She made a wish on a shooting star that this perfect weekend would never end. But when she woke up Monday morning, she knew the fun was over; it was time to go home and face the music.

When my dad dropped my mom off, both her mom and Tom were in the house waiting for her. The second she walked in the door Tom started calling her a filthy whore and told her to get all of her shit out of his house immediately. My grandma was crying and told her how disappointed she was, and that she was an embarrassment to the whole family. My mom began crying and felt horribly guilty; she didn't want to hurt Tom or disappoint her mom. She just didn't know how to tell them that she didn't love him anymore. But, fortunately for her, by this point she didn't have to tell him; he said he wanted a divorce immediately. That was music to my Mom's ears. She was now free to be with my dad.

Two days later my grandfather walked my mom and Tom to his lawyer's office where they signed their divorce papers. When all the legal formalities were finished, my grandpa took them out for an ice cream cone to celebrate their divorce. Even though Tom was heartbroken, he understood that my mom loved him as a friend, but just not as a husband. They ended on relatively good terms and were always cordial in the following years when they would see each other in public.

Six hours after signing her divorce papers, my mom began moving the few things she owned into my Dad's trailer. She hated his trailer because it was always a mess. The dishes were never done and there was laundry all over the floor. They threw parties nightly so there were always empty beer bottles in every room. My mom wasn't working at the time so she would occasionally try to clean the place up, but most of her time was spent lying in bed watching soap operas and resting up for the next party.

Like most relationships, the first couple months were a lot of fun. But as the days went by, my mom started to see the less charming side of my dad. She noticed that he was no longer sweet and funny when he drank. He became a mean and violent drunk who would frequently disappear for hours at a time.

The first red flag was the time she had a dental emergency and needed his help, but he was nowhere to be found. One Saturday morning after a long night of partying, she woke up and her mouth was hurting. She called the dentist, a family friend, and asked if he could squeeze her in immediately. When she got to the dentist's office he took one look and saw that she needed to have her wisdom teeth pulled. He told my mom that she would need to have somebody drive her home after the procedure. She called my dad's trailer, his job and his brother's house and nobody had a clue where he was. She then called her mom, who had to leave work to pick her up. Instead of taking my mom back to David's trailer, she took my mom to her house so her little sister Talla could take care of her.

Hours later, my dad called my grandparents' house (very drunk) to ask where she was and when his dinner would be ready. My mom was still drowsy and could barely talk, so she just replied, "Fuck you" and hung up the phone. Twenty minutes later, she was lying on the couch in the back living room when she heard a huge crash in the front of the house. Before she could even stand up to see what was going on, David was standing over her. He was screaming at her, saying he would fucking kill her if she ever hung up on him again. My drunk asshole dad had busted down the front door. Luckily my mom's little sister heard all of the commotion and ran downstairs to see what was going on.

When she saw David screaming at my mom, she picked up the phone and started to call the police. My dad saw her dialing, ran over and yanked the phone out of the kitchen wall. He put the phone under his arm and walked out the front door yelling over his shoulder, "Let's see you hang up on me with no phone, you stupid bitch!" When he got out to his car, he spiked the phone like a football in the middle of the street, and sped off.

My grandparents were furious when they came home from work and saw the destruction. They sat my mom down and told her that she should stop seeing him immediately. They were worried that he would kill her one day. My mom agreed and said she was done. She asked if she could stay at their house for a couple of weeks, and then she would get her own place. My grandparents told her she was welcome to stay as long as she needed to, they just didn't want her to spend one more night at David's trailer. That didn't last long. The next morning my dad came over with two-dozen roses and an apology card. The apology worked, because my mom took the roses with her back to his trailer that night. After this incident he was back to his sweet, charming ways for a couple months. Then, out of nowhere, everything changed. He became very possessive every time he got drunk and accused her of cheating on him. If she even said hello to one of his friends, the second the guy walked away David would say things like "I know you want to fuck him, just go fuck him, you fucking whore!" My mom wasn't cheating on him and most of the guys that he brought around were repulsive. She was getting tired of his abuse. A couple of times she felt like he was close to hitting her. She talked about it with all of her friends and decided for her own safety she had to leave him. She made up her mind that she was going to spend one more week with him while she waited for Candy's roommate to move out.

SURPRISE
PACKAGE

That last week of living with him in the trailer, she found herself feeling sick every morning when she woke up. She figured it was just anxiety; she knew David was not going to take the news of her moving out well. Every day she geared up for what she was positive was going to be a huge fight when she tried to leave. But then one morning Candy called and said, "Maybe you aren't feeling well because you are pregnant." My mom panicked. "No way!" She drove to the grocery store and bought three pregnancy tests, hoping that they would all come back negative. After the first two came back positive, she didn't even bother taking the third test.

And that is the beautiful story of how I was created.

The moment my mom found out she was pregnant, she was convinced her parents would freak out if she had a kid out of wedlock. So, seconds after telling my dad he was about to be a father, she also informed him that he was also about to be a husband. My father was ecstatic about both scenarios, and immediately called everybody he knew. That is the beautiful story of how my parents became engaged. My mom and dad were both worried about telling

 their parents, but really they had nothing to worry about because both sets couldn't wait to be grandparents. Who doesn't love grandkids? Even if they are made irresponsibly by two people that have no business being together? My mom's parents said they could get married at their house and everybody began planning a beautiful May wedding.

Some of my mom's friends were not as excited and voiced their concerns. They reminded her that it was just last week that she wanted to dump his drunk, lazy, no good ass. My mom now defended my dad. David was, in fact, a great guy, and she said she was just being dramatic. In my mom's defense, she did say that my dad became very sweet and caring the second she told him she was pregnant.

The first two months he stopped partying every night and would come home right after work and take care of her. He was picking up extra shifts at work and taking a break from all the drinking and drugs so he could save up some money. Knowing he had a son on the way, he decided to rent a nice house in the middle of town and get his family out of the trailer park.

David rented a charming two-bedroom house with a huge kitchen and a beautiful backyard. My mom finally felt like they were a happy little family. Unfortunately, that feeling would only last a couple more months. About 4 months into her pregnancy, a bunch of the railroad wives came to my mom and told her that David was constantly cheating on her. She didn't want to believe it, but they taught her how to check the train schedules and she quickly found out that he wasn't picking up overtime shifts on the nights he said he was. They also told her that he had been married prior to meeting my mom. This really upset my mom, because my dad told her that he had never been married, and he was so excited to have a wife. She called my grandmother. She didn't mention the cheating rumors, but did tell her that David had been married before and asked her what she should do. My grandmother told her that if she was going to marry David, she should call his ex-wife and find out why it didn't work out. My dad hated this idea, but my grandma put her foot down and said that she would not let her daughter get married unless she talked to my dad's first wife. My grandma now had two phones in her house

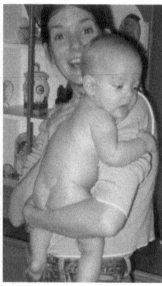

(so if some asshole came and pulled one out of the wall, she could still call the police.) She got on one phone and listened while my mom called David's ex-wife and asked her about their past.

My dad's first wife warned her that David was a liar and a cheater. She regularly found letters and pictures from strippers and other women who lived all over the world. She also said that he never took responsibility for his actions, nor was he responsible with money, and was very immature. Her final words were, "I don't think David is the marrying type." This was just the ammo my grandma needed, and from that day on she did everything she could to try to keep them apart. She told my mom over and over that my dad was going to ruin her life. She begged her to hold off on the

wedding, telling her she wouldn't be mad at all if she had a child out of wedlock. But there was no changing my mom's mind. She wanted to get married and she wanted to do it before she got pregnant and fat. She wanted to look good in her dress, and she did. My grandfather said, "That day she looked like the most beautiful girl in the world."

Unlike my mom's first wedding, they decided to have an intimate wedding in my grandparents' backyard. Both families were there and my mom still says it was the perfect night. The first few months of married life were great. My dad calmed back down and was coming home every night after work to help my mom decorate the nursery. After weeks and weeks of hard work, they had the house all ready for a baby. I decided that September 23rd, 1977 would be the perfect day to make my grand entrance. My mom was walking around the mall with my grandma and her younger sister that morning when she felt her water break and knew it was time to get to the hospital. My dad was at work at the time, but luckily, he was on a train that was only 15 miles out of town. As soon as the train got back to the station his boss informed him of the good news and he rushed to the hospital. He made it to the hospital just in time to see the most handsome and healthy baby boy come into this world. I made it out of belly-jail and I was excited to meet all my new family members.

I was the first grandchild so, needless to say, I was spoiled rotten. David was a great dad from day one, but unfortunately, it didn't take long for him to become an awful husband. He started cheating on my mom again about three months after I was born, and this time he was not even trying to be sneaky about it. With a newborn baby, he figured my mom couldn't leave him even if she wanted to. My mom would constantly get phone calls from her friends saying they saw her husband out with other girls. To solve this problem, my dad decided to move our family 50 miles south to Ft. Collins, Colorado. He would then commute to Cheyenne on the days he had to work. This was his way of isolating my mom from her friends and family. If she couldn't talk to anybody, then nobody could tell on him. My dad wouldn't let my mom get a house phone, to assure that nobody could give her updates on his whereabouts. We also only had one car, so when my dad would leave for work, my

mom and I would be stuck at home with no transportation. Sometimes he would be gone for two or three days and my mom and I would have to make the two-mile walk in the cold to the grocery store to get baby food and diapers. My mom hated her life and was very depressed. She felt trapped and knew something had to change. After a year of living unhappily in Ft. Collins, she finally stood up to my dad and said she was moving back to Cheyenne.

After threatening to leave my dad for good, he managed to use his charm to convince her to give him one more chance. He found a nice rental house near my grandparent's house and we moved back to Cheyenne. My mom loved living close to her parents because they were always willing to babysit. After a year of being alone, she finally got a little time to go out and get her social life back. She loved occasionally going out with the girls, and once a week having a date night with my dad. My dad, was once again, trying to be a good husband. He would come up with something new and interesting each week for them to try. One cold Friday night in late October, my dad told my mom he wanted to introduce her to his new best

friend. She had heard how much fun his new best friend
was and she was excited to meet him. That night my dad
introduced her to cocaine. That little white powder made
a very strong first impression with my mom. She loved it.
After that night, they were doing coke and drinking seven
nights a week. This was very hard on my mom. She was
staying up late partying, and then had to take care of me
all day long running on very little sleep. She became very
frustrated with my dad because he was not helping with me
or with anything around the house. He would wake up, go
to work, and begin drinking and getting high on his drive
home from work. The cheating finally stopped, but that
was only because all of his thoughts were about when he

could get high next. She asked him to stop doing drugs or at least slow down, but he didn't listen. He never listened.

My mom had a few long conversations about his substance abuse with her mother, and my grandma told her that now was the perfect time to get away from him and end this marriage. She assured my mom that my dad only cared about doing drugs, so he wouldn't care if she left. My mom agreed and decided that sometime in the next week she would sit him down and tell him that she wanted a divorce. Three days later when she woke up, she felt nauseous and went to the bathroom and vomited. She started to panic and thought, "Please just be stress. Don't tell me I am pregnant again." Just like the previous time, she rushed to the store and bought three pregnancy tests. This time she took all three tests. And they all came back positive. She was officially pregnant... again. This made her rethink her plan of leaving my dad. She didn't have a job and was scared to death to try to raise two kids by herself. She knew she could move back in with her parents but the thought of raising two babies in a tiny basement bedroom seemed like an awful idea. She decided she was going to stay with my dad during the pregnancy, hoping that, with a second child on the way, he would realize it was time to grow up. When she told my dad the news he was excited. It was cause for a celebration. Cocaine for everybody! Once my mom found out she was pregnant, she knew she had to quit smoking, drinking, and doing drugs immediately. And while the party stopped for her, it did not skip a beat at our house. Knowing that he would soon have another mouth to feed, my dad decided that not only would he start doing more cocaine, but it was also time to start selling it. My mom said he started going to work at the railroad less and less and spent all day selling drugs out of our home. The foot traffic coming in and out of our house was constant from 10 AM to 3 AM every day.

Every morning my dad started the day with what he called, "Champagne and Cocaine Brunch." This was a term my dad insisted he had invented and it was very popular among his friends. My mom said they all loved to yell it any chance they got: "CHAMPAGNE AND COCAINE BRUNCH, BABY!" My dad would leave the house every day around 5 p.m. and go to the strip club to pick up more drugs and get drunk with his brother. Unlike the first pregnancy, my dad was no help at all this time. He had lost all interest in being a husband and a father. That was never more evident than on June 9th, 1979, when my little brother Ryan Lawrence Tobler was born. My grandma tried to get a hold of my dad all morning, but he was nowhere to be found. My mom gave birth to my little brother all by herself that day. Of course, my grandparents and I were there, but nobody from my dad's side of the family made it to the hospital.

The following day my dad showed up and told my mom some bullshit story about why he couldn't make it, but all we knew the truth. He cared about his strippers and blow way more than his family. At this point, everybody in my mom's life was begging her to leave him. When my dad felt the backlash from everyone, he knew it was time to stop selling drugs, slow down the partying, and put the charm back on. My mom forgave him again. Just like she did every other time he treated her like shit. But everybody around her wasn't forgiving him this time. My mom's family and friends had had enough. They started following him into bars and letting all the women know that he was married. And my grandpa was driving to the railroad lot each day to make sure he was really at work when he told my mom he was.

Feeling like he was constantly being watched, he decided it was time to pack us up and move out of town again. He told my mom that he got transferred to Ft. Collins and that we had to move back. About six months after my little brother was born, we packed up a big U-Haul truck and moved back to Colorado. My grandma tried to talk my

mom out of it, but my dad had a power over my mom that nobody could ever contend with. We moved to a nice little two-bedroom house at the bottom of a mountain on the west side of town. My dad immediately started selling drugs again, and this time was making a lot of money. My mom said he would have tens of thousands of dollars in cash, but would complain every time she asked for a couple hundred dollars to get stuff for the house.

Once again, he wouldn't let her get a house phone, and we still only had one car, so we could only leave the house if we were going somewhere with him. It was just like the last time we moved to Ft. Collins, but this time things were even worse. My mom had to walk even further to get to a grocery store, and now she had to load up two little kids. All that charm had worn off, and she hated him. He was now very mean to her every chance he got. He began to physically abuse my mom, and when he would finish beating her, he would scream at my little brother and me, telling us what a "cunt" and "fucking bitch" our mom was. We obviously didn't know what those words meant, but even at two years old I knew the words were bad. My mom said she hated seeing the way my face would react to his tone and how I would sneak off to my room and cry quietly when my mom was crying and upset.

The morning after one of the worst beatings, my mom remembered waking up next to my passed-out dad. As she laid there, bruised and sore, she had only one thought in her head: "If I had a gun I would kill this mother-fucker right now." This thought really scared my mom. She was very anti-gun and anti-violence in general, so she couldn't believe she was having thoughts of blowing her husband's brains out. She said that was the moment she finally saw the light, and knew she had to get away from my dad for good. She told herself she would sit down with my dad when he woke up and tell him that she wanted a divorce and needed him to drive us back to her mom's house in Cheyenne.

My dad finally got up around 1 PM that day and stumbled downstairs to the living room. My mom was sitting at the kitchen table feeding my little brother.

"David, I need to talk to you."

"We will talk tomorrow, I have to go to work."

"You don't have to work today, I need you to take us to Cheyenne right now."

"For what? What the fuck you gotta do in Cheyenne?"

"We gotta get the FUCK away from you!"

My dad didn't like that answer. He went over to the kitchen table and put my mom in a headlock, dragging her into the living room. He then began banging her head on the metal front door. He was now screaming, "You want to leave me? Well just open the door and leave then bitch!" After slamming my mom's head six or seven times, he let her go and she fell to the ground. As she lay there screaming and crying, she heard a knock on the door. My dad then started to open the door, but couldn't get it all the way open, because my mom was lying there. He kicked her in the ribs and said: "Move bitch, so I can open this mother fucking door." When he opened the door a man my mom had never seen before was standing there and he glanced down at her. My mom was lying there crying and covered in blood and the man didn't even acknowledge her. He looked at my dad and said: "Let's go, baby. It's champagne and cocaine time." My dad stepped over my mom and slammed the door as hard as he could on his way out. As my mom lay there in pain, she suddenly thought of a sign she would always pass by at the grocery store. It had a picture of a woman with a black eye and it said, "If you are the victim of physical abuse from a boyfriend or husband, stop living in pain and fear. We are here to help." It had a phone number at the bottom of the poster. She had to get to that poster.

She packed up a stroller and diaper bag, and loaded everything she could on top of the stroller. We walked almost three miles to get to the grocery store. My mom said she was scared the whole walk; terrified my dad would drive by and see us. When we finally got to the store, she wrote down the safe house number and went outside to the pay phone to call them. After three rings a very sweet older lady answered and asked if my mom was okay. The lady then asked if she would like them to send somebody to pick us up. Within twenty minutes a nice couple pulled up in a station wagon and got out of their car and introduced themselves. They both gave my mom a big hug and reassured her that she was safe. My mom, my brother, and I climbed into the rear seats and they loaded the stroller and our stuff in the back. We then drove downtown to a beautiful old Victorian house. When we went inside there were two older gentlemen who checked that we were all physically okay before taking my brother and me into a big playroom full of toys. My mom loved the house and hoped we could stay there for a while. Unfortunately, the ladies in charge of this safe house sat her down and gave her the bad news. They had a rule that people could only stay two nights. They gave her some options on where and what she could do after the two nights were up. My mom didn't have a plan and wasn't sure what to do next. She really didn't want to call her mom who had told her a million times to get away from David. She couldn't stand the thought of hearing her mom say "I told you so." But, with no other options, my mom decided

to swallow her pride and make the call. My grandmother hopped in her car the second she hung up the phone, and made the fifty-five-mile journey to North Ft. Collins to pick us up.

My mom said they didn't speak for the first half of the ride home, but as they crossed the border back into Wyoming, my grandma turned to her with tears in her eyes and said, "Why do you keep doing this?" My mom replied that she loved him, to which my grandma snapped back in anger, "What can you possibly love about him? Tell me right now exactly what it is that you love about him?" My mom asked herself and realized that she couldn't come up with a thing. They sat in silence the rest of the way home as she stared out the passenger window, trying not to cry. That night my mom stayed up all night tossing and turning in my grandparent's guest bedroom, nervously waiting for David to show up. She knew he must have been furious when he got home and that he would head straight to Cheyenne to find his wife and boys. Surprisingly, my dad never showed up that night, and the next day he was still nowhere to be found. A few days later my mom found out that the only thing that stopped my dad from driving to Cheyenne and creating chaos was that he had been locked up in county jail. My dad's mom, my grandmother Mildred, called my grandmother's house and asked to speak to my mom. My mom was very hesitant to take the phone call. She assumed she was going to get yelled at for leaving town, but that was not the case at all. Mildred begged my mom to talk to David. He was in jail and refused to talk to anybody but his wife. When my dad came home and saw that we were gone, he decided it would be a great idea to get wasted and drive around town looking for us. After hitting four parked cars, his Cadillac went airborne and ended up landing on the roof of a fifth car. My dad didn't have any serious injuries, but was arrested and taken to jail. With my grandma sitting right next to her, listening to every word, my mom told Mildred that she had nothing to say to David; she never wanted to talk to him again.

After that conversation, my mom didn't hear anything from my dad or his family for almost a year. During that time, my grandfather hired my mom to be the secretary at his appraisal company. My mom loved spending time with her dad every day. He was a sweet, generous, and hard-working man who put a smile on the face of every person he interacted with. My mom occasionally thought about David, but she didn't miss all the ups and downs. She spent quite a few nights lying awake in bed, worrying about my brother and me not having a father-figure around as we grew up, but after everything she'd been through, she was in no hurry to start dating. After about eleven months of not seeing or hearing from my dad, she answered the phone at work one day and immediately recognized the voice on the other end of the line. It was him, and he asked if he could take her out to a nice dinner. My mom initially said no, but my dad was relentless and begged and pleaded. He wanted an update on his boys, and he couldn't wait to tell her about his new job. He swore that he was sober, working hard, and was ready to be a good father. He told her to put on her best dress, because he was taking her to the best Italian restaurant in all of Colorado. My mom eventually agreed to go, but told him she couldn't go until the following week. She needed a little time to come up with a story to tell her parents, because she knew they would freak out if they found out she was going on a date with the man that had caused her so much pain. That night when she got home from work, she asked her mom if she would mind babysitting my brother and I next Friday night. My grandma said, "Of course! What do you have going on?" My mom told her that one of her old high-school girlfriends was having a birthday party in Ft. Collins. My grandma told her that sounded like a lot of fun, and since she hadn't gone out in months, it was a great idea.

A week later, as the sun was going down, my mom and dad discreetly met up in the back parking lot of a Kmart. When my dad pulled up, my mom quickly snuck out of her car in a short black dress, and hopped into my dad's brand new red Ford Mustang. My dad took the back roads out of town, assuring nobody would see them. When he made it to the highway, my dad floored it and they were doing 105 mph, passing everybody in sight. As they flew over the Colorado border, my mom was full of excitement. She realized this was going to be their first-ever romantic dinner. My mom said they had a great time on the forty-five-minute drive. My dad was making her laugh and still had that undeniable charm that had attracted her the first night they met. When they got to Ft. Collins, my dad told her they had to make a quick stop at his friend Rob's house. He told my mom that he always talked about her, and wanted to introduce his stunning ex-wife to his new best friend. "We gotta put a beautiful face to all of my stories." This made my mom blush, and for the first time in a long time she was feeling butterflies in her stomach; she loved it. My mom had no idea who Rob was, but she assumed this new best friend was partly responsible for my dad's new job and sobriety, so she couldn't wait to meet him. She quickly found out that was the furthest thing from the truth.

Within seconds of walking into Rob's house, my mom saw eight people sitting around his dining room table drinking and playing cards. Rob was sitting at the head of the table and my dad brought my mom over and introduced her. Rob stood up and shook my mom's hand, saying, "It is a pleasure to finally meet you!" He invited them to sit down and join the party. Rob then walked into the kitchen to grab some more beer for the game. When he came back he had a twelve pack of Coors Light in his right hand, and a small silver pipe in his left hand. He set the box of beer down in the middle of the table, and sat back down in his seat. He then lit up the pipe and took a big hit. After taking the hit, he leaned his head back, blew the smoke towards the ceiling, and then passed the pipe to his right. As the pipe slowly made its way around the table, my mom was curious to see what my dad would do when the pipe got to him. This would be a real test to his "living sober" lifestyle. When the pipe got to him, he didn't hesitate to hit it and then pass it to my mom. My mom was never good with peer pressure, and with a table full of people staring at her, she took a hit. After hitting the pipe, my mom started coughing uncontrollably. She felt an awful burning feeling in her chest and weird tingling in her legs. She had no idea what she had just smoked, but she knew she hated it. They stayed at Rob's house partying until almost midnight that night, totally missing their dinner reservation. My mom told my dad she had to get back to Cheyenne, because she promised her mom that she would be home by 2 AM. My dad didn't want to drive her back to Wyoming. He was having fun partying with his friends. My mom begged and pleaded and finally his friends told him to take her home. On the car ride back, my mom was feeling sick and asked what had been in the pipe they all smoked.

" It was crack. Didn't you love it?"

"No, I hated it! And I thought you told me you were sober now!"

"I honestly tried to be sober, but I just love living my life in the fast lane. Don't you love the fast lane? I feel alive when I am going fast. I just want to go faster and faster!"

"You are right David, I love it! The fast way is the only way to live."

Those were the words coming out of her mouth, but in her mind she was thinking something much different. She knew that drive would be the last time she was ever alone with him. She was a mom raising two little boys and had no business being in the fast lane. She agreed with him out of fear, and her only thoughts were getting back home safe to her children. When they got back to Cheyenne he dropped her off at her car, and didn't even put the car in park to say goodbye. He kept his foot on the brake as my mom got out of the car, and the second she shut her door, he sped off so he could get back to Ft. Collins and continue partying. As my dad drove off, I think he realized it was over too.

After that night my mom didn't hear anything from or about my dad for almost eight months. Then one morning, while reading the paper, she came across an article saying that my dad and three of his friends had been arrested on drug charges. A few months later he was sentenced to three years in the United States Penitentiary in Leavenworth, Kansas.

My mom didn't tell me any of these stories until much later in life. Like most kids, I thought my father was the best dad in the world when I was a kid. Luckily my mom did her best to try to protect my brother and me from the shitty things going on around us. I have very few bad childhood memories of the early years with my dad. Honestly, I don't really remember anything before the age of five… and from the sound of it, that is for the best.

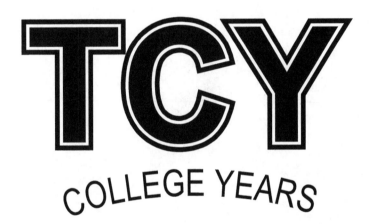

THE

TCY

COLLEGE YEARS

When I think back, the first memory I have is of my mom telling me that my dad wouldn't be around for a while because he was going to college. College, that's what my mom called it; normal people might call it the slammer. I guess you could say my dad had a full ride scholarship because the state was paying for his room and board. I remember telling all my friends how smart my dad was and that he was going to college at Princeton. I assume my mom told us Princeton because it sounded a lot like prison. I was seven and my little brother was five, so we had no idea that Princeton was one of the most prestigious colleges in the country. We would get a weekly collect call from "the university" and my brother and I each got to talk to my dad for five minutes. Looking back, I should have easily figured out where he was. One hint was that every year on his birthday and Father's Day we weren't allowed to get him presents. My mom always said we would just send him a little money for his books. I thought it was for actual textbooks; I didn't know we were putting money on his books so that he could buy stuff from the commissary. We weren't allowed to get him power tools, golf clubs, or awful ugly ties like my friends

Two Sentenced to Prison For Cocaine Distribution

Two narcotics suspects were sentenced to prison terms of 5 and 8 years, respectively, when they appeared today before U.S. District Judge Ewing T. Kerr.

David L. Tobler of Cheyenne drew the 8 year sentence to a federal prison facility on his plea of guilty to a charge of distribution of one pound of cocaine March 3 in Laramie.

Kerr sentenced Robert L. Spaulding of Fort Collins to 5 years on his guilty plea to an identical charge.

The U.S. attorney said the two men sentenced today were among five defendants in the same case where arrests were made by agents of the Department of Criminal Investigation. A spokesman for the attorney noted that Linda Carter of Cheyenne was placed on probation for three years last week by Judge Kerr on a misdemeanor charge of possession of cocaine.

The cases of the five who were arrested in Laramie were presented to a grand jury here with indictments issuing from that jury March 19.

were buying their fathers. Our second-grade class project was to make boxer shorts for our dads. We got to paint them however we wanted. The boxers I made for my dad had a big red heart on the back and on the front, they said, "I love my daddy." My mom said that she never sent them to him, but I think they would have gone over well in prison! The crazy thing was that even though he was in prison, he still managed to kind of get us everything we wanted for our birthdays and Christmas. When my brother wanted a bike, he got a Kansas license plate that said BMX. I loved the Denver Broncos and really wanted a Nintendo, so I got license plates that said Nin10do and L-way. My bedroom was covered in Sports Illustrated covers, license plates, and a big red stop sign. It was just like sleeping in an Applebee's. To this day, when I see vanity plates on cars, I wonder to myself: "Is that driver's dad in prison?"

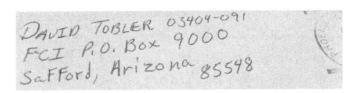

DAVID TOBLER 03404-091
FCI P.O. Box 9000
Safford, Arizona 85548

Every couple of years my dad would randomly show up unannounced and visit us on his spring break. It was really weird when his spring break would fall in the middle of winter. My mom said that the real story was that he would never call ahead to let her know he was out of jail; he would just show up out of nowhere and ask if he could see us in an hour. My mom wouldn't let us go with him alone, so he would end up taking all three of us out to lunch or dinner. We would have a great time during the meal and my dad would always promise that he would stick around for a few days to watch whatever sports games we were playing that weekend. I remember always playing poorly those weekends. Not because I was nervous that my dad was there, but because I spent the whole game staring into the bleachers hoping he would show up. My dad had a Cal Ripken streak of not showing up at our games. I think he missed 2,000 in a row. Luckily for my brother and me, around my dad's sophomore year in "college," my mom met a new guy named Ron.

It was a slow Monday morning at my grandfather's office and my mom looked up from her typewriter when she heard the bells on the front door jingle. In walked a handsome six-foot-four man with a big smile on his face.

He strolled over to my mom's desk and introduced himself. Ron was new in town from Maryland, and a friend suggested he check my grandfather's office for a job. My grandfather hired Ron three days later, and Ron began to flirt with the boss's daughter every day. Ron thought my mom was one of the most beautiful girls he had ever met. After working with her for about six months, he finally got the courage to ask her out. My mom said yes, and they begin casually dating for the next seven months. My mom was in no hurry to introduce another man into our life, but after knowing Ron for over a year she started slowly bringing him around our house. My brother and I immediately fell in love with Ron. We rejoiced anytime he came over to our house. He would take us to the park and play football and basketball with us for hours. After months and months of seeing him almost daily, one day he took my brother and me to Dairy Queen as a reward for getting good grades. After getting our ice cream, he sat us down and asked us both if it was okay if he married our mom. We couldn't say yes fast enough. He was a great stepdad, and I think we both needed that with the absence of our father in our lives. Ron would coach our sports teams, teach us how to ride bikes, and take us on family vacations all over the country.

Two years after getting married, my mom and Ron would have my beautiful little sister Hayley. I was ten years old when she was born, and I instantly become her protective big brother. Hayley was one of the cutest kids ever. And as she grew up, just like Ron, she never missed

one of our games. She was our favorite little cheerleader. We had the perfect family and I rarely thought about the fact my real dad wasn't around. My dad would call every couple months and tell my mom he would kill Ron if he ever did anything to his sons. My mom was trying her best to ignore his violent threats, so my frustrated dad decided it was time to call Ron himself. He called Ron at work one day and said, "Motherfucker, I am going to kill you when I see you." Ron, in a very calm and collected voice that showed he meant business, said, "I don't think that's going to happen." After that conversation, my dad never said another negative word to or about Ron. My dad was a bully; and once Ron stood up to him, my dad treated him with respect from that day on. I would also imagine that deep down inside my dad knew that Ron was good for us.

Over the next couple years, my dad continued showing up sporadically without any warning. We would usually see him for a couple of hours two or three times a year. As we got older he would come around more often because my mom would let us spend the entire weekend with him. My dad had a new parenting style, and it was to spoil us for a few days and then get the hell out of town. My brother and I were now eight and ten, and we loved it because we could get our dad to buy us anything and everything we ever wanted. My dad was selling drugs again and always had a huge wad of money in his front right pocket. Feeling guilty for never being around, he would tell us over and over how sorry he was that he missed all of our games and important events. He told us he really, really wanted to be there, but he had to get his education. He would constantly remind us how important it was that we did well in school, so one day we could grow up and be just like him.

Whenever he visited Cheyenne, he would stay at the Thunderbird Hotel. It was a seedy forty-five-unit dump, located directly across the street from his favorite bar. When we stayed with him it was always the same routine. We would walk up the block to the convenience store where he would give us each a one-hundred-dollar bill and we would buy a ton of soda, all of the candy we wanted, and a couple boxes of baseball cards. He would then lock us in our hotel room and tell us he had to go meet with one of his professors across the street at the Chinese restaurant. He would then go to the bar and get drunk

with his friends. He would come check on us every couple hours and make sure we were okay and see if we needed any more junk food. My dad literally hired Cherry Coke, Starbursts, and Topps baseball cards to babysit us. My dad only had young, blonde, female professors and we would meet a new one every night after their dinner. I can't tell you how many drunk women would come in and tell my brother and I that we were so ridiculously cute. We knew more women in Cheyenne than the Mary Kay cosmetics rep. If my mom and Ron had known what he was up to, they would have never let us spend the weekend with him. But I was never going to tell them because we loved those weekends with our dad. He could never tell us goodbye, so he would drop us off back at home on Monday morning and tell us he would see us later that night. Every time, without fail, "spring break" would end abruptly, and my

mom would tell us that our dad was so sorry he didn't get a chance to say goodbye, but he had to hurry back to college to work on his master's degree. It was good for our bodies and teeth that he left, because I don't think it's particularly healthy for growing boys to eat seven-hundred Starbursts and drink a two-liter bottle of soda every night.

The difference between Ron and my dad was literally night and day. One of them was responsible and worked hard all day long, and the other one refused to work and slept all day long. I learned so much from Ron and so little from my dad. For instance, Ron led our Boy Scout troop, showed us how to throw a curveball, and helped us perfect our multiplication tables. He taught us all the stuff boys needed to know. This was important because my dad was teaching us all the stuff he knew about. These things may have been useful in his life, but they were things we probably didn't need to know.

Looking back, I realize that my dad told us all kinds of bullshit. For some reason there are three things he said that, while I don't really agree with, I have never forgotten.

Rule number one: you never snitch. You never ever snitch, no matter what. Even if somebody told on us, we were taught to never snitch on them. "Nobody wants to hang out with a rat. Rats always die alone and only a coward tells on another man." Rule number two: if you have extra food at lunchtime, you only give it to white people. As ridiculous as this was to tell a ten-year-old boy in the first place, it was never really an option. Where I went to school, 95 percent of the students were white, and I was a growing boy so I always ate all my lunch. The third and final rule was the most absurd, but it's something I still think about at least once every day. It was a hot summer day in the middle of July, and my dad took us swimming at the Cheyenne Municipal pool. We spent almost three hours playing Marco Polo and jumping off the diving board trying to make one-hand catches. My dad had finally worn us out, and we decided it was time to hit the showers. My dad was flirting with the young blonde lifeguard all day and he stopped to talk to her before heading into the locker room. My brother and I rushed to the showers and were getting cleaned up as fast as we could because my dad had promised us Red Lobster for dinner. We were so excited because we loved crab legs, and my dad would always let us get the "all you could eat" special when he was in town. As we were getting ready to get out of the showers and dry off, my dad walked in and told us to pay attention because he was about to teach us something that would help us the rest of our lives. He said, "Boys, every time you take a shower from now on, before you get in the shower, put the water on as cold as it can go and then get in that freezing cold water and shadow box until you count to fifteen." It sounded like fun, so my brother and I both shut off our showers and then tried it. The second we stepped into that ice-cold water, we both immediately jumped out screaming. Puzzled and cold, I asked my dad why he told us to do that. He said, "Son, the way your body reacts when that cold water hits it is the same way it will react if you ever get stabbed. So, if you ever get shanked, you will be able to fight back for at least 15 seconds." That's the advice he had for a ten and twelve-year-old. We were just kids in elementary school. Nobody was going to stab us on the playground at recess. But he was our dad and we believed everything he told us, so like an idiot, from that day on, I started my showers like that. I did it every day until I was nineteen and had a girlfriend who started staying over at my place. She was so confused about why we had to fake fight in freezing cold water every morning. I told her, "Babe you gotta stay ready," to which she replied, "You better stay ready to find a new girlfriend if you ever make me do that again!"

I think my dad hated that Ron was such a great stepdad. It was obvious that he was very jealous of the relationship my brother and I had with him. He would always say, "Yeah, Ron is a great guy, but he will never love you as much as I do." My dad's favorite saying was, "Blood is thicker than water, Son. Always remember blood is thicker

than water." He must have said that to my brother and me a thousand times when we were kids. I always hated that dumb phrase. My dad made a ton of mistakes when we were growing up, but instead of giving us the apology we wanted and deserved, we had to hear that annoying saying over and over. "Oh, I missed your birthday again. Sorry son. Just remember blood is thicker than water." My dad eventually found a way of dealing with his jealousy towards my brother's and my relationship with Ron. He started making us promises that he would buy us whatever we wanted. That is the easiest way to assure that your two kids think you are way cooler than their stepdad. He would tell us both to put together our wish list and if we didn't get in any trouble and had good grades, he would send us a package with the stuff on our lists at the end of each month. My brother and I were ecstatic every time we got off the phone with our Dad because it was like having Christmas twelve times a year. We would be on our best behavior every day and do our homework every night, and at the end of the month, we would rush home after school each day to see if our package had arrived.

Later in life, my mom told me that for the first two months my dad did keep his word and sent us the packages. But the third month he got arrested again and was sent back to prison. Obviously he couldn't continue buying us stuff while in prison, but that didn't stop him from promising us that our package was on its way. My mom and Ron didn't want to see us disappointed and were afraid we still weren't old enough to understand that our dad was a liar and not actually in college, so they would go buy all the stuff my dad had promised us. They'd have to go to the UPS store (less than a mile from our house) and mail a package to our house making it look like it was still coming from our dad. Every day we would run home from school and anxiously sit on the front porch in hopes that the UPS truck would come and deliver our presents. You could always hear and see that big brown truck from blocks away, and as it got closer and closer, we would get more and more excited! As soon as the truck parked in front of our house, we would run up and grab the package from the driver and then tear it open in our front yard. It shows what great parents my mom and Ron are because we would immediately invite all of our friends over to play with our new toys while raving about how cool our dad was for always getting us everything we wanted. To make things worse, my dad would call us each week and my mom and Ron had to listen to us thank him over and over, telling him that he was the best dad in the

world. My mom said she would scream at my dad and tell him to quit promising us stuff that he couldn't deliver. My mom and Ron didn't have the money to buy us a bunch of stuff that we didn't need each month. A normal person would thank my mom for covering for them and then back off from making promises they couldn't keep. But not my wonderful dad. He made things worse.

Once my dad found out my mom was covering for him, he just started promising us more expensive gifts. It was a total free roll for him. He would promise us all kinds of stuff and see what my mom would actually end up getting us. My parents couldn't afford elephants and Lamborghinis and all the other crazy stuff my dad would promise, and they decided they had to put an end to this charade. They told my dad that they would not buy another thing and say it was from him. My dad is such an asshole that he just kept saying he was sending packages. When they didn't show up, we would ask what happened and he would promise us both that he sent them. He would tell us that there was a mix-up at the post office, but he got it straightened out and our presents should be at our house any day now. My brother and I would ride our new scooters home every day (the ones our dad supposedly bought us) and wait for the UPS man to bring our new stuff. But now the UPS man was just driving by our house and never stopping. My brother and I would ask our mom daily where she thought our packages were, and if she could call UPS because there had to be a mistake. At this point, my mom and Ron were done covering for David so they started telling us that they didn't know where the packages were, but if my dad had really sent them, they should have arrived by then. I would argue with them that there was no way my dad hadn't sent them. He had promised, and Dad never lied. I was convinced they were lost somewhere in the UPS warehouse.

After three months of pestering my Dad about where our packages were, he finally had an answer. At this point, he could have easily told us the truth, but instead, he told me he had no clue where our packages were, but he had a sneaky suspicion that the UPS guy might be taking our packages home and giving them to his children. To a kid, this theory made perfect sense. The UPS man did see us open the other packages the second we got them, so he knew they were always full of cool toys. For the next week, I laid in bed every night thinking about our missing packages. I was convinced that the UPS man had stolen our stuff and I came up with to a plan to get it all back.

The plan was this: instead of rushing home every day to see what the UPS man had delivered, we would wait for the truck to pass by and then follow him. We would follow him on his entire route, and then continue following him back to his house when he got off work. If we got there and found his kids playing with our toys, we would shank them and take our stuff back. We had been taking our cold showers every morning; we were ready for a knife fight. Of course, my brother and I needed knives, so we rode our bikes up to the Owl Inn restaurant, which was the "fancy" diner located five blocks north of our house. We parked our bikes behind the restaurant and walked around to the front, entering through the double doors. When we entered, we asked the hostess if we could use the bathroom. On the way, we each grabbed a steak knife from the pre-set tables, and sprinted out the back door. We hopped on our bikes and rode home as fast as we could. When we got to our house, we hid the steak knives under an old board in our tree house. We weren't sure how many kids the UPS man had, or how big they were, so I made the decision to recruit two of our neighborhood friends to go with us. My brother and I decided to ask Eric and Jeremy Mead if they were willing to help us in what might be a fight to the death.

The Mead brothers were very close to our age and notorious in our neighborhood for causing trouble. They were considered legends for kicking over trashcans, egging people's houses, and shitting in library books and putting them back on the shelf. Needless to say, we didn't have to ask them twice; the chance to shank a couple of kids was an opportunity they couldn't refuse. The only day they couldn't go was Thursday, because Eric had a dentist appointment. Two days later the Mead boys came over after school, and we climbed up into our tree house and made our plan of attack. We decided that Friday after school we would follow the UPS truck all the way to his house and then peek in his windows to see if his kids had our stuff. Now, if you think running with scissors is dangerous, try bunny-hopping curbs with a steak knife in your hand. We are lucky we didn't kill ourselves within a block of our own house.

That Friday afternoon, the four of us went straight to my house the second school let out. We waited in the backyard until we heard the big brown UPS truck on the next block. We jumped on our bikes. The truck rounded the corner and the chase was on! We followed that truck for almost two hours that day. We went up and down his whole route with him, but in the end, he didn't end up at his house. He eventually made it back to UPS headquarters where he parked his big brown truck in the far corner of the lot. We watched him get out of his work truck, lock the driver's side and big back door, and then got into a green jeep and speed off the lot. "FOLLOW THAT JEEP!" I shouted. To our chagrin, the driver didn't live close to headquarters, and he lost us within minutes of pulling out of the gates. UPS guys are a lot harder to follow when they are not stopping every three houses. In retrospect, this was a gift. I wasn't ready to go to "college" at the age of twelve. Once we realized the hunt was futile, we rode our bikes to the park and threw the steak knives into the lake so the police would never find them. Jeremy and Eric advised us that we had to do that because that's what they always do in the movies after they kill somebody.

About a week after our Tour de Force attempted-murder bicycle trip, my mom sat me down on her waterbed and handed me a manila folder. I opened it up, and it was full of newspaper clippings about my dad's many arrests and his sentencing. As I began to read them, my mom said, "I am sorry I lied to you, Son. Your dad was not in college this whole time. He is in prison. He will be calling some time tonight to explain everything and to apologize to you and your brother. He will also answer any questions you might have." I stomped out of the back door, climbed up the ladder to the tree house and broke down crying. Ron climbed up after me and sat with me for an hour, trying to calm and comfort me. He told me that my dad wasn't a bad person; he had just made a few mistakes. He assured me that my dad loved my brother and me more than anything in the world.

That night, I sat in my bedroom and waited for my dad to call. I wanted to ask him why he did these bad things and make him promise me that he would never get in trouble again. My dad did call that night, but there was no time for an explanation or apology. In fact, I never even got to ask him a question. He was upset, and very passionately insisted that Ryan and I couldn't take Ron's last name. We were Toblers, and we would always be HIS sons. He kept saying, "Never forget what I always tell you—blood is thicker than water, Son, blood is thicker than water." During our phone call, I had no idea what he was talking about. When I got off the phone, Ron sat my brother and I down and told us that he loved us and was so happy to be such an important part of our lives. He said he was honored to be able to help raise us for the last seven years, and considered us his own sons. He told us how proud he was of the young men we had become, and that he would be honored if we would take his last name and let him legally adopt us. That conversation was very confusing for the two of us. We both felt Ron was like a dad, but we also knew he wasn't truly

our dad. Looking back on
that day, the whole thing was
rough on us. We had woken
up still assuming that our dad
was the best dad in the world,
and hours later we found out
that was very far from the
truth and that he lived in a
maximum security prison.
Everything was happening
too fast.

I think my mom and Ron realized that there was a little
too much going on in our little brains, so they told us we
could sit down as a family and talk about the adoption thing
in a day or two. Ron told us there was no hurry, and there
was nothing to worry about because they would be happy
with whatever decision we made. I knew it was going to be
a really tough choice for my brother and me to make. We
loved both our dad and Ron, and as young kids, we didn't
want to upset or disappoint either of them.

Luckily, my brother and I never had to make that
decision. My dad decided to make the decision very easy
for all of us. He began having his low life friends call Ron
at work each day and threaten to kill him if he ever tried
to adopt David Tobler's sons. He would tell anybody
who would listen, that Ron's last name would be on a
tombstone in the Cheyenne cemetery before it was on any

legal document following the words Brandt and Ryan. After a month of my dad's daily phone calls and countless threats of violence, we sat down as a family and decided that my brother and I would just keep our last names.

In all honesty, this is the one and only time that my dad came through for us in life. As much as I loved Ron and did consider him my dad, there was no way I wanted to start junior high as Brandt Hufendick! That's right, my stepdad's name is Ron Hufendick. I am not sure there is a worse last name for a junior high kid to have. After the decision was made that my brother and I would stay Toblers, my dad just disappeared. The weekly phone calls stopped coming and I don't remember hearing from him once during my junior high years. We would get birthday cards from him some years, but I have a suspicion they came from my grandparents. My dad's penmanship and grammar seemed to improve a lot in two years. Dad not being around during those years was perfectly fine with me. I had Ron. My brother and I also had the advantage of growing up in a small town, so everybody knew about my dad's troubles. We were fortunate to have great coaches and teachers that went out of their way to make sure my brother and I were okay and had positive male role models in our lives. With Dad gone, my new problem was Mom.

My mom also had a secret life that she tried to keep from us. Unlike my dad, she was not interested in selling drugs, but she still enjoyed using them. I would routinely catch her sneaking around our house, smoking weed. Now as an adult, I realize it was not that big of a deal, but as a kid, I thought it was the end of the world. I had just finished the DARE program, and Nancy Reagan told me that I had to Just Say NO to drugs! Unfortunately, the DARE program doesn't teach you that there is a huge difference between black tar heroin and marijuana.

Our DARE program was built on regular visits by a police officer who visited our sixth grade class and tried to scare the shit out of us by screaming stuff like, "If you do drugs you will end up dead or in prison!" After just finding out that my dad was in prison, the DARE program made me think that if my mom kept smoking weed, she was going to die. It was crazy in our house because we had reversed roles of most parents and junior high kids. My mom was sneaking around smoking weed, and I was always snooping through her room trying to find it.

And just like a worried, nosy mom, I would always find her stash, and start crying, and yell at her. "You are going to ruin this family! Don't you know you are going to end up dead or in prison!"

My first week of 8th grade, a teacher pulled me aside and said: "You smell like marijuana. Have you been smoking?"

"No."

"Well, this better never happen again, or I will be calling your mother."

I remember rolling my eyes and thinking, "Oh yeah, my mom will certainly be shocked." The last thing I wanted her to do was to call my mom; not because I would be in trouble, I just knew it would ruin my mornings, because it would make my mom spray on more cheap perfume before she took my brother and me to school. My friends all smelled like Drakkar Noir cologne, and I smelled liked Piña Colada Passion Paradise. Seeing how upset her drug use made me, my mom eventually began really going out of her way not to smoke anywhere near our house. I was no longer finding any drug paraphernalia in her room, and I couldn't catch her in the act no matter how hard I tried.

When I got to high school, I watched a ton of my friends get busted for using drugs. I realized that none of them were dying or going to prison, so I gave up on trying to catch my mom. In hindsight, my Mom smoking weed wasn't that big of a deal, especially now that marijuana is pretty much legal in most of the United States. Later in life I asked her why she continued to do marijuana even though it upset me, and whether Ron got mad when she did it. She told me that it really helps with her anxiety,

and Ron loved to do it with her occasionally, so he didn't care. But those moments did have a huge effect on me, because to this day I have never done a drug in my life. My DARE certificate is framed and hangs up in my office to this day. It's mostly to make my friends laugh, but I did take an oath in 6th grade saying I will never do drugs, and I think I might be the only one from my class to never break that oath. Another reason I chose not to drink or do drugs in junior high or high school was that I was convinced I was going to play division one college basketball and then go to the NBA. It was a ridiculous dream for a 5'11 white guy from Wyoming, but I was always told by my teachers and coaches to dream big. I think what they actually meant was that I should have dreamed that I was bigger. I would have needed to grow at least another 6 inches if I ever wanted to make it as a pro basketball player. But being small never stopped me, and I always believed I could make it to the pro's when I was a teenager. I was starting point guard

all through junior high school and spent every free hour I had on the playgrounds working on my game. In the summers my life revolved around basketball. My friends and I would wake up and immediately head to the courts. We would play all day long, and the games wouldn't end until we literally couldn't see the ball. Somebody would always get hit in the face with the ball, get a bloody nose, and that was our sign that it was time to head home. On the way home, we would grab some food, go to one of our basements, and watch basketball videos until we fell asleep. What I loved about basketball is that on the rare occasion that I did miss my dad, or when I was super upset about my mom doing drugs, I could always escape that world by going to a court and shooting hoops. I played thousands of imaginary games against Michael Jordan, Magic Johnson, and Larry Bird. My parents both have very addictive personalities, and I think I am the same. Lucky for me, I was only addicted to basketball.

Unlike a lot of kids, I really enjoyed junior high. The older kids in my neighborhood really liked me, so I had the luxury of coming into junior high pretty popular. This is the first time in my life I realized that I was funny, and quickly learned that I could win strangers over by making them laugh. I was voted class clown my 9th-grade year, which, to me, was the coolest award in the yearbook. Looking back, I really miss those days. Life was easy, and I was having so much fun. I spent all day shooting hoops, making people laugh, drinking Cherry Cokes, and eating chili-cheese hot dogs. People would occasionally ask me about my dad, but at the time, I was so happy that I rarely even thought about the fact he wasn't around and was making no effort to be a part of our lives. As I got older and started to mature a little bit, I realized I didn't need my dad in my life. If he didn't want to be a part of my life, that was okay, because I was surrounded by people that did. And as much as I loved junior high school, when I got to high school, things got even better.

Early in my sophomore year, I made friends with Andy Pannell. Andy was one of the "cool" seniors, and we hit it off immediately. He was the senior guy that everybody liked and respected. What impressed me the most about Andy was that he was genuinely nice to everybody he met. This is something you rarely see in any high school. At the start of the school year, cliques are being formed, and teenagers are trying to find themselves and figure out who they are. Andy was very confident in who he was, and I watched his every move. He always seemed to make the right decision, and I was taking notes, because I wanted to be just like him. That first month of tenth grade, he took me under his wing and taught me everything I needed to know about high school. Simple things like where to go to lunch, where to hangout before and after school, and which teachers to avoid at all costs. And best of all, he let me go with him to all the senior parties. These parties were full of cheap whiskey, cases of Keystone Light beer, and all of the hot cheerleaders. Most of the popular seniors got drunk daily. They were drinking before school, during lunch, and in the parking lot the second the school day ended. There was, and still is, not much to do in downtown Cheyenne, so getting wasted is most people's idea of fun night. It can be very depressing during the long winter season, when it gets tough to leave the comfort of your warm home. Most high school students and adults just get drunk in different basements each week. Andy didn't drink or do drugs, so even though we hung out with the party crowd, we always stayed sober. At that time, most of my sophomore  friends were caving into the peer pressure from the popular seniors, and they started experimenting with drugs and drinking heavily. Meanwhile, my only thoughts were on the basketball season, and my high school career got off to a good start when I made junior varsity as a sophomore. The best part of basketball season was the road trips. Wyoming is a huge state, so we would have five or six-hour bus rides every other week during the season. There was nothing better than being on a marathon bus ride with 45 of your best friends after a victory. I would give anything to go back and take one more trip with that team.

That first year of high school flew by, and before I knew it, I was watching Andy graduate and head off to college. I was really going to miss Andy. He knew about everything I went through growing up, and really went out of his way to be a positive influence in my life. I knew my junior year would not be the same without him. When my junior year started, I no longer cared about going to the cool parties or hanging out with the hot girls. I was only focused on one thing, and that was being the starting point guard on the varsity basketball team. Andy and I talked a lot about setting goals, and that was the first real goal I had ever set for myself. I worked my ass off morning, noon, and night, and was determined to beat out the seniors in front of me. And when tryouts came... I did it!

Becoming the starting point guard my junior year was the biggest thing that had ever happened to me. Andy was right, you set a goal, and then you work hard every day to make it happen. The morning of our first home game, my mom woke me up to show me that my picture was on the front page of the local paper. It was such an amazing feeling to see my family so proud. That picture was immediately on the fridge at my aunt's, grandparents', friends', and most importantly, our house. Our games were played at the legendary Storey Gym that was located just blocks from my house. As a kid, I had watched my local heroes play there every Friday and Saturday night. From the ages of five to fourteen, my friends and I would sneak into that gym every chance we could. I had spent countless nights dreaming about the day I would get to play in front of a sold-out crowd. That first game, when the PA announcer called my name during the starting lineups and I got to run out to half court and hear the roar of the crowd, I literally had to fight back tears. It was such an emotional moment for me, but the

last thing I wanted was all the hot girls and my opponents to see me standing there crying. We won our opening game that night and after starting a little shaky due to my nerves, I ended up having a pretty good game.

After accomplishing my goal of being the starting point guard, I knew I needed a new goal. I decided my next goal would be to get a girlfriend. Honestly, that was always a little part of the starting-point-guard goal. I figured if I was the star basketball player, all of the girls in school would want me. Most of my close friends had girlfriends, but I was definitely a late bloomer when it came to dating. I was always the kid at the party covered in sweat, from playing ping-pong and jumping on the trampoline all night. Meanwhile, all of my friends were dry-humping cheerleaders in basement closets. The nights always ended with them asking me, "Yo what's wrong with you? Why didn't you try to make out with that girl, she likes you." I was terrified of rejection. I had this constant fear that I would close my eyes and try to kiss a girl and at the last second she would turn away, and I would slam my open-mouthed face into her ear. This was something I would wake up in a cold sweat thinking about many times my sophomore year.

Midway through the basketball season, we won a big game against our cross-town rivals, and I finally got my first kiss. It was that romantic moment we all dream about for our first time. You know, when the drunk sophomore girl is staring at your forehead and says, "Are you going to kiss me or what?" and so you say, "YES" a little to loudly and come flying at her face with your tongue all the way out, spinning like a tornado. It was not my finest moment, and I knew that immediately because I heard the girl's friends outside the window laughing hysterically as they watched the whole disaster. I eventually did get a girlfriend late in my junior year, and I fell in love fast. Her name was Molly, and she was one of the many cute and funny sophomores. I was introduced to her as the girl that likes your little brother. I figured, well, if she likes my nerdy little brother, she would love me. And I was right. We started dating and immediately started spending every second together. Neither of us had done anything sexually, so we got to go through that whole awkward experience together. We dated through the summer and into the next school year. I was so excited to start my senior year. I had the perfect girlfriend, and I was sure our basketball team was going to be great. My goals were to be All-State, win the state championship, and then go through all of my scholarship offers and pick the best university for me. I really wanted to go to Duke, but was also thinking I might go somewhere in California, because I wanted to be near the beach. I was mainly interested in the schools that had a lot of nationally televised games. I wanted my girlfriend and family to be able to watch every one of my games back in Wyoming. Unfortunately, my dumbass head coach had a much different plan for my senior year. He took away my starting spot and benched me after the 5th game. He felt like I was our leader, and since we weren't winning, it was my fault. This crushed me, because I was, by far, the best point guard we had on the team. Somehow, I got lost in the politics of high school sports. The hardest part was being on the road, and having the opposing fans and coaches ask me why I wasn't playing a lot that year. They were grateful, because they remembered me just killing them the year before. My coach was a legend in our community, but the game had passed him by, and he wasted a team with a lot of talent. He retired after that season, but if you ask me, he stuck around one year too long. I often dream about what would have happened if I had gone to our rival school across town. Getting benched my senior year hurt more than anything I had ever gone through. Basketball was my first love, and I had dreamed of having a great senior season and then heading off to college to continue playing. Obviously, the college coaches weren't exactly beating down the door of a guy that averaged five points and couldn't start for his shitty team in the hoops hotbed that is Wyoming. When the season ended, I fell into a deep depression. Not only did my basketball coach decide I wasn't good enough, so did my girlfriend. She started cheating on me with one of my closest friends. There were only a few months left in my senior year, and I decided it was time to focus on my schoolwork, so I could try to get into a good college. I found out very quickly that it's hard to get your 2.3 GPA up to a 4.0 when there are only three months of school left. I actually almost didn't graduate, because I got caught cheating on one of my finals.

This is how lazy and stupid I was: I got caught cheating in art class. I was sad and pouting around, and had no interest in doing my big senior project, so I turned in my friend's incredible drawing that he had gotten an A on earlier in the year at his art college. When I handed my final drawing to my teacher, she was shocked and furious. She said she had never felt more disrespected. She watched me turn in absolute shit all year long, and then I turned in a

masterpiece. She just looked at the picture, and said, "Are you serious? Brandt, you have not turned in anything half this good all semester long, and now you are turning in this?" She sent me to the principal's office, where I quickly confessed and apologized. The principal told me that in his 30 years of working in the school district, this had to be the dumbest thing he had ever seen. I remember him asking me, "If you were in a music class, would you have tried to dress Garth Brooks up like you and have him come in and take your guitar final?" I told him of course not, a music teacher would never fall for that. He just shook his head and (thankfully) said, "Mr. Tobler, I am going to let you graduate. Just don't be a jackass at the ceremony and make me regret my decision."

A week later, I walked across the stage with my fellow seniors. I had a huge, shit-eating grin on my face the whole ceremony, and I couldn't believe I did it. I survived high school! I got my diploma, and my family was so proud of me. The week leading up to my graduation, my grandparents had promised me that my dad would be there. But on my big day, once again he was nowhere to be found. Honestly, I don't remember what bullshit excuse they gave me, because I never believed for a second he was going to actually show up. Fool me once shame on me, fool me for the 340th time, I must be an idiot that can't figure out that his dad doesn't give a shit about his sons. I didn't need him, I was now a high school graduate, and I was ready to conquer the world. I just had one little problem... I had no idea what I was going to do next.

THE Mafia

Three days after graduating, my mom and Ron sat me down and told me that I better spend my graduation money wisely, because they were done financing me. I was still more than welcome to live with them, but I needed to get a job. My friend Rachael worked at a pizza parlor in the mall, and she had gotten a couple of our friends jobs working with her, so I asked if she could help me out. Rachael was nice enough to vouch for me, and a week later, I was offered a part-time job making delicious pizza on nights and weekends. It was official: I had my first real job, and it was at Parkway Pizza, the best pizza place in town.

The restaurant was run by four Italian brothers that had just recently moved to Cheyenne from New Jersey. Now, I am not claiming they were in the Witness Protection Program, but I am not sure why the restaurant had 15 video cameras, a shotgun in the freezer, and cocaine was a secret topping you could get if mall security was not around. It's fair to say that they did business slightly different than your hometown Pizza Hut. Every Sunday, their 5'4" father would come into the restaurant in impeccable designer suits.

He was an older man, probably in his early 70's, and he had an air of confidence about him I had never seen in our little town. I was fascinated by Geovani. He would sit at the end of the bar, talking to his four sons, individually, for hours. I would always try to eavesdrop on their conversations, but they only spoke in Italian, so I had no idea what they were talking about. After watching his every move for a couple months, I was convinced that he was the head of the mafia. He was just so cool. The way he walked, talked, and dressed all blew my mind. I had never seen anything like it in real life. He was just like the mob bosses I had seen in my favorite movies. I had to resort to movies, because prior to getting the job, I don't think I had met any Italians. We had more pizza toppings at work than Italians in my small, very white town. I decided that my new goal in life was to be in the Italian mafia. Over the next month I read every mafia book, and watched every mob movie. I came to the realization that

the dream of being an NBA
star was impossible for a 5'11
white guy from Wyoming,
but the dream of being a
5'11 white kid in the Italian
mafia was very, very possible.
Fuhgeddaboutit! Obviously, I
am a very unrealistic dreamer.
I waited and waited to be
invited into this tight knit

famiglia, but no dice. Eventually, they fired me because I
was rooting for team USA against Italy in the World Cup.
Oh, and it probably didn't help that I was late for work a
bunch of times. When I got fired, I was back to square one.
I had no real plan, and I didn't know what I was going to
do next.

Luckily, when I worked at Parkway Pizza, at the end
of the night, we were allowed to take the unsold pizza
home if we wanted it, but I got so tired of eating pizza that
I had started to give it to the guys who worked next door
at Sports Fan. We became pretty good friends over time,
and they offered me a job the same day I got fired. I was
now working in a very relaxed sports apparel store, which
was the perfect job for me. Before, I would often times
spend half of my pizza paychecks at Sports Fan. Now I
could do the same thing, but with a 25% discount. We sold
fitted baseball hats, football jerseys, and all kinds of sports
apparel. The job itself was super easy, and when the store

wasn't busy, we just watched Sports Center and threw the football around the store. I always loved coming to work. My bosses at the store were extremely laid back, and they pretty much let me do whatever I wanted. That fun time was short lived.

After a couple months of working there, the corporate bosses started showing up every couple of weeks, and they treated us all like shit. Here is a lesson for business owners: if you treat your employees well, they will spend all day trying to help you beat the competition. If you treat them like shit, while you are spending all day trying to beat the competition, they will spend all day trying to figure out how to beat you. After constantly being yelled at about stuff that was totally out of my control, I decided it was time to not only work for them but to also start working for myself. I started to really pay attention to how things were run in the store, and it didn't take me long to find some major holes in their system. That's when I decided to take all of my mafia knowledge gleaned from the pizza joint and start what I called the Mallfia!

Here is how the Mallfia worked: if you worked at Taco John's and gave me tacos a couple times, I'd give you a hat. You work at Foot Locker and give me some new shoes, I give you a jersey. You work at Sears and give me a TV, I give you one of everything we have for your favorite team. The store did inventory once a year, and I knew I was on a free roll until that week came. I figured I would just quit a couple weeks before they decided to do inventory, and the corporate assholes would then figure out that the Godfather hit them for a big score. After five months of hustling, I had the Mallfia running so strong that I could get anything in the mall except puppies, jewelry and cinnamon rolls. A Mormon family owned the cinnamon roll store and they were not giving anything away, which was fine because they were shitty cinnamon rolls anyway. I walked around the mall like John Gotti, and it felt so good to be treated like the king.

Everything was running smoothly, until one day, the high school girl that worked at the clothing store directly across from Sports Fan decided to snitch on me. She had traded me a couple pairs of plaid boxers for a Lakers championship hat for her dad. I guess the guilt was too much for her, because the next day she came in crying and spilled the beans while I was on my lunch break. Of course, you remember what my dad said about snitching. And I know when it happens in mob movies, somebody always gets whacked. So I knew technically I was supposed to kill her, but I definitely was not ready to commit a brutal murder in the middle of the food court of a mall. Instead, I decided I would send my message by getting a bunch of rotten eggs and leftover food from the Country Buffet and throwing it all over her house and car. That is how I got my Mallfia revenge. Now the big problem was going to be dealing with the corporate managers at Sports Fan, whom I despised. They made the 100-mile drive up from

Denver to scream at me for over an hour, and then they let me know that I was fired. They said they knew I was giving away their merchandise and that they weren't going to press charges. Oh, and also, even though I was fired, they needed me to work one more week. I was so confused. They then explained to me that since it was December 20th, they didn't have time to train somebody new to handle the pre-Christmas rush and the after Christmas returns, so they really needed me for one more week. So basically, I was technically fired, but I would continue working until December 28th. When they told me that, I immediately lied and said, "Of course I will help you guys. It is the least I could do since I gave away a couple of things." In my head, all I could think was, "Oh my god, everybody I know is going to have the best Christmas ever!"

During my final days, I, of course, would give all of my friend's stuff, but I also loved hooking up random little kids with hats and jerseys. It felt awesome to be a real-life Santa Claus. What I didn't realize is that when you are an adult and a stranger, you can't just give little kids free stuff. I would let kids pick a free hat, and they would run out of the store so happy. Five minutes later their dad would stomp back in and ask me, "Why does my son have a new hat?"

"Because I gave it to him, I am Mallfia Santa Claus!" I would reply, while wearing a big red Santa hat.

"No, you are a pedophile. Quit giving my kid free stuff, you creep," the dad would reply.

I quickly realized I should leave the Santa duties to jolly old guys. The good news, though, is that I was able to hook up a few single mothers, and that made me feel awesome. I didn't tell the moms that I was blatantly stealing the stuff for them because I knew most of them wouldn't take it. Instead, I would tell them that I got a 75% discount for working there, and they could use it on whatever they wanted. They would cry tears of joy because I was able to give them the stuff their kids really wanted, instead of them only getting their kids the stuff they could afford. I know what my mom went through as a single mom, so I will never forget those interactions. Watching those moms smile and cry, knowing how much these gifts were going to make their kids go crazy on Christmas morning are moments that I will never ever forget. As I write this, I am tearing up, because it really was an amazing feeling to make somebody else so happy. That's what Christmas is all about, right?

Eventually, the 28th came, and I was actually fired. The Mallfia was over, and I had to go back to regular life. I didn't go to college that first semester after I graduated, because I didn't have the money and didn't really know where I wanted to go. All my friends were at different colleges all over the country, and they were calling me and sending me pictures telling me how much fun they were having. I decided I needed to get my ass to a college ASAP! After spending hours thinking about which college I should attend, I finally made the tough choice to pick the only school I could really afford and that would accept me. It was the junior college in my hometown, the very prestigious Laramie County Community College, or LCCC for short (which everybody in Cheyenne said stood for Last Chance Community College). It was a white Soviet-esque bunker, located about eight miles south of my high school in a field in the middle of nowhere. The only thing near it was an oil refinery that made the campus smell like rotten eggs. I was essentially going to 13th grade with the other local losers I had been going to high school with the last four years. The only difference was we all showed up hungover for class, unlike high school when only half of us showed up still a little drunk. I decided I would major in physical education.

My youth had been blessed by so many wonderful coaches and teachers that really had a positive effect on me, and I wanted to someday do the same thing. Another thing that motivated me to get a teaching degree was how easy those college courses looked. I figured as a high school P.E. teacher, all I would had to do was throw out a bag of balls each class and tell the kids to have fun and don't get hurt. Seemed like the perfect job for me. When I was in high school, I dreamed of playing college basketball, but I didn't even get to try out for the basketball team at LCCC. This was, in part, because I was now a 5'11, slow, white guy, but, mainly, it was because the school didn't have a basketball program. The only sport the school offered was rodeo. Some of my favorite college nights involved getting drunk and going to the arena to cheer on our rodeo team. There were always huge crowds, because we had one of the best rodeo teams in the nation! I had drunk visions of trying out for the rodeo team, but the only event I had the courage to try was barrel racing, and it's only for girls.

All of my free time was spent with my two best friends, Casey and Tim. I had known both of them for over a decade, but when we all three enrolled at LCCC, we became inseparable. We had three things in common that really sealed our bond. We loved beer and basketball, and hated our dads. They both had fathers that had also chosen to be a very minimal part of their lives, and the drunker we got, the more we vented about our dads. We had each other, and we were convinced that was all we needed. The three of us did everything together, and that included dropping out of college after one semester on the same hungover Monday morning. We decided the curriculum was just too hard, and we couldn't focus on our education when we had fake IDs and no curfew. After taking the spring semester off getting drunk and chasing girls, I took a summer job babysitting my friend Jill's little brother. This was the perfect summer job, because I could show up in the morning and sleep off my hangover on the couch, while he played with the other neighborhood kids. Jill would leave us money for lunch every day, so after my morning nap, we would go get some fast food and then sneak into a hotel pool and swim the rest of the afternoon. I wish I could have made this a career, but as summer came to an end, my little buddy had to go back to school, and I figured I should probably do the exact same thing. I decided that fall that I needed a second chance at the Last Chance Community College, so I re-enrolled. This time, I didn't even make it two months.

After six weeks of expensive books and boring classes, I was out of there! College was such a waste of time for my friends and me. None of us had any idea what we really wanted to do, and we just weren't that mature. We would do stupid shit, like put up pictures of bestiality on all the computers, so all the real students had to see a giant horse having sex with a small girl before they could check their email. That was hilarious to us. Looking back, I can't believe what losers we were. We would much rather do childish pranks than study for our exams. We spent countless hours gluing quarters to the cafeteria floor, and then laughing uncontrollably when people would try to pick them up. We thought we were so funny, and everybody else on campus thought we were so stupid. I obviously wasn't ready for college. I think I only went, because I thought that's what I was supposed to do. College definitely is not for everyone. I think I still have eight credits, if anybody wants them. Six of them are P.E. credits, but they should transfer to any junior college in Wyoming. The crazy thing is, I actually do have a college degree.

Yes, it is a real degree! It clearly states that on December 11th, 2004, Brandt David Tobler graduated from the University of Wyoming with a bachelor of science and a minor in business management. I know you must be wondering how this happened. Well, I earned that degree by having romantic relations with the Assistant to the Dean. Her job was to write the names of the graduates on the degrees, and lucky for me, they had a couple extra degrees laying around, just in case she made a mistake. Most people spend thousands of dollars on college and end up owing student loans for the next 20 years. Not me. My degree cost me two big bottles of Captain Morgan Rum, an Applebee's dinner, and four minutes of mediocre sex.

My friend Casey and I both got degrees, and we thought it was a great idea to have a big graduation ceremony in his front yard. We invited our families and a bunch of our unimpressed friends. My neighbors owned the local Coors Light distribution center, and they donated two kegs to the party. The promise of free beer made a lot of people show up for our big day. We didn't have caps and gowns, but we did try to make it at real as possible. Everybody did the Pledge of Allegiance before the ceremony started. We then had our drunk friend, Leo give a commencement speech on what not to do in life. It wasn't a motivational speech like most graduations; it was him slurring stories full of curse words about all the people that ruined his life. There was a six by six stage built of bricks that we stood on when we received our diplomas. And after our mothers handed us

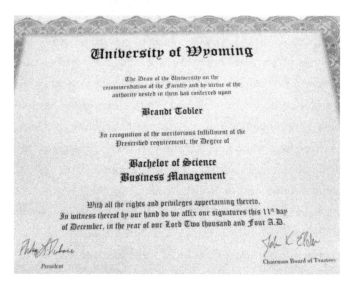

both our diplomas, we turned our backward baseball caps to the front, then took them off, and threw them as far as we could. Our moms were so proud of us, and both ended up getting way too drunk and emotional. Neither of them graduated from college, and they both kept saying how beautiful the ceremony was. My mom even teared up a little bit. The whole thing was absolutely ridiculous, but also hilarious. To this day, that college degree hangs proudly next to my DARE certificate on the wall in my office. One day, I will tell my kids about the hours and hours of studying and homework I had to go through to get that degree, and to just say no to drugs!

After dropping out of college that second time, I once again had ambition and wasn't sure what I was going to do next. All I knew was that school was definitely not for me, and I needed to make money. I missed that power and respect I once had when I was the kingpin of the mall. I decided I had to get another job in the mall, and this time, I was going to take the Mallfia to another level. At the time, I had a friend that worked at the clothing department store, Dillard's, and after grilling him about the store's operations, I was amazed by how shitty the place was run. I went in and applied, and on the application I made it look like it would be my first job (I had a feeling Sports Fan and Parkway Pizza would not be great references). Dillard's was notorious in the community for treating their employees terribly, and they consistently had a high turnover ratio. They called me in for an interview, and one week later, I was on the sales floor plotting my takeover. If you know anything about Dillard's, you know it's a huge department store that had no business in Cheyenne, Wyoming. Dillard's was very expensive, and most people in Cheyenne are hard-working people that don't really care about designer brands. I am not sure how they expected us to sell anything when there was usually nobody in the store. All of the employees had a weekly quota that was impossible to hit. When you didn't hit your quota, the department manager would question how hard you were working and tell you that you needed to be more aggressive when somebody walks into your section.

They put me in the Ralph Lauren section, so I was trying to sell $80 polo shirts, but that was extremely challenging, given that there was a Target 200 yards away selling the same shirt for $18. Wyoming people were of the mindset that because they had real horses at home, they didn't care if there was a little horse on their shirt. So, after months of not meeting our quotas and constantly being yelled at by some idiot rich guy they moved in from corporate, I had no problem convincing my eight coworkers in the men's department to join my criminal enterprise. The Mallfia was BACK!! It was very easy to run the whole operation at Dillard's, because they didn't have any security cameras. The only security they had was an on-duty Cheyenne police officer in full uniform patrolling the store. For a real cop, this was an awful job. He would always show up late, take long lunches, or sit in his car and sleep. When he actually was in the store, he spent all day and night at the front entrance, hitting on the make-up girls. I could see the front of the store from my cash register, so I always knew what the cop was doing. The men's department was huge, and my coworkers and I had stations about 25 yards away from each other, so I came up with a bunch of silent hand signals to communicate with the other employees when the cop was patrolling the store. If I gave the signal that the cop was up there hitting on the girls, the back door cashier told my friends they could walk in and out of the back of the store with as many bags as they could carry. The Mallfia was now unstoppable. As the boss, I could now get anything I wanted anywhere in town. I now not only had access to men's, women's, and children's clothing, but I could also get everything from luggage, shoes, and even

housewares. I was very generous with all of Dillard's stuff, and I made sure everybody I knew in Cheyenne was looking good. My friends loved it, because most of us grew up poor and couldn't afford the expensive Tommy Hilfiger and Nautica stuff that was hot at the time.

I decided I was only going to wear Ralph Lauren, and after five months, I had at least one of every Ralph Lauren item we had in the store. Every color shirt, every style of pants, I even had four Polo belts. I was a 20-year-old kid with maybe $800 in the bank, but a $40,000 wardrobe in my closet. Needless to say, I was looking good, and I feeling even better. But then, one day, it looked like my luck had run out. I came to work and there was some weird guy who was pacing around the store for a couple hours but didn't buy anything. Although we all tried to help him, he repeatedly told us he didn't need any help, he was just looking. My Mallfia instincts told me something was definitely wrong. I gave the hand signals to everybody working that day to immediately shut the whole operation down. Of course, my instincts were right, because later that afternoon there was an announcement over the loudspeaker: "Brandt Tobler, please report to the office. Brandt Tobler, please report to the office immediately."

My first thought was to walk out the back doors, get in my car, and leave forever. But as the announcement ended, I saw everybody in the mens' department look at me to see what I was going to do. At that moment, I knew I couldn't run. I was the Mallfia boss! Would John Gotti run? Never! Did Al Capone leave his soldiers behind? I don't think so. So, I held my head high, and I began my slow walk down to the office. Everybody came from behind their cash registers and walked to the front of their sections. My section was furthest from the office, and I had to walk by all of my crew on my way to meet my fate. Not one of them said a word to me as I walked by. I could tell they were with me in spirit, but I could also feel that the whole store was scared. When I got to the office, they took me into a huge conference room that I didn't even know existed. It was a dark room with no windows, just a long table right in the middle of it. On one side, there was one seat that the police officer said was for me, and on the other side, there were five seats. As I sat down on my side of the table, the police officer walked out and closed the door behind him. I sat in that room all alone in silence for about 25 minutes. Suddenly, the door flew open, and in charged the head of the mens' department, the head of the womens' department, the general manager, the Cheyenne police officer, and the guy that had been walking around the store all day. They introduced the guy as the Head of Loss Prevention, and they informed me that he had flown in from Dillard's headquarters in Little Rock, Arkansas just to meet me. They all sat down at the table, then the head of the store went into high school principal mode. He kept saying, "If you just tell us the truth we will go easier on you." And I kept saying, "I don't know what you're talking about." This just made him progressively angry, so he got louder and louder. Finally, he was screaming, "WE KNOW WHAT YOU HAVE BEEN DOING. JUST TELL US THE TRUTH AND WE WILL GO EASIER ON YOU!" As you remember, the first thing my dad taught me was that you never, ever snitch! So, I kept saying I had no idea what he was talking about. Eventually, the head of the mens' department told me they saw my girlfriend walk out of there with two bags full of stuff last Tuesday. "That's not true," I said, "and if it were true, then why didn't you arrest her? You saw her steal a bunch of stuff, and you just ignored it?" They all looked at each other confused, and nobody really had an answer for that question. Now I was gaining confidence, and I felt like I had the upper hand.

What I didn't realize was that they still had one more trick up their sleeve. They pulled out five envelopes that I immediately recognized as letters I thought were being sent to one of my best buddies, Chance, who was at Navy basic training. When you work at Dillard's, you are supposed to send thank-you notes to your customers to build a relationship, and then, months later, send a follow-up letter to keep them updated on the fall and spring collections as they come out. But, I wasn't selling anything, so I was sending my letters to Chance, who I knew was very homesick while stationed in Mississippi. I just assumed he didn't write back because he was busy learning military stuff and doing push-ups, so he could defend our beautiful country.

When I saw the head of the store pull out the letters, I snickered a little bit, because I knew what I had written in them. Chance was a couple of years older than I am, and I always looked up to him, often asking him for advice. I was 20 years old when I wrote those letters, and I had just started having sex with a few girls, so those letters were full of crazy stories and questions. You see, I had never had a cavity in my life, and then I started going down on girls, and the next time I went to the dentist, I had eight cavities. So I was asking Chance crazy questions like, "Does eating pussy give you cavities? Am I doing it wrong? Does it matter if the girl is Mexican? Are Mexican vaginas like piñatas and full of sweet candy?"

The loss prevention guy saw me giggle when they brought out the letters, and it really pissed him off. He stood up and pounded his fist on the table and screamed, "Hey kid this isn't some kind  of joke! We did inventory, and this store is off $600,000 dollars!" I was absolutely shocked. I couldn't help but think," holy shit, my dad would be so proud of me! I really am a Mafia boss." My Mallfia was definitely responsible for a lot of that loss, but there is no way we stole over a half million dollars worth of stuff. Obviously, everybody else in town also knew about their lack of security. After the loss prevention guy had finished yelling at me, the general manager pulled one of the letters out of it's envelope and asked what one of things I had written meant. All of the stationary had the word Dillard's imprinted on it, and on one of the letters I wrote "I am robbing DILLARDS blind. I have so much stuff for you when you come home!" I didn't actually write the word Dillard's, but it did happen to fit just perfectly in the middle of my sentence, where I had written it on the letterhead. The exchange went something like this:

The general manager started pointing at it, yelling, "What does this mean? Tell me what this means!"

"I don't know what you are talking about."

"It says you are robbing us blind,"

"I didn't say you guys, the word Dillard's just happened to be there." I tried to tell them that I was talking about Sports Fan, my old job. I told them I had stolen a bunch of stuff from there for him before they fired me. They didn't believe that lie for one second, and they were then quick to point out even if that were true, why wouldn't I also be stealing from them. It was obvious to everybody in the room that I was probably guilty, but I knew they had no real evidence of me actually stealing anything. I continued to say I had no idea what they were talking about. And that just made them more upset. I knew I didn't want to continue arguing with them, so I decided I had to take a stand. I stood up, put my hands behind my back, and said, "I am done talking. Fire me or arrest me."

The head of the store screamed, "Sit down! We are not done talking to you!"

"Well I am done talking to you, so fire me or arrest me!" I replied.

They all looked at each other, and the cop said, "Let's step out of the room for a second." They stood up, visually upset, and shuffled out into the hallway. On his way out, the cop gave me a glare and told me to sit down, because they would be back. I sat alone in that conference room for what seemed like forever. I remember my legs wouldn't stop shaking. At that moment, I realized I was nothing like John Gotti, I was a  scared kid that just wanted to go home. All I could think about was that my friend Matt had been caught stealing over $500 worth of stuff from Disc Jockey, and had received a felony conviction. If I had stolen over $600,000 worth of merchandise, I would be in jail forever. I am never going to get another cavity! Finally, the general manager came back in, with only the cop following him. His face was bright red, and you could tell he was furious. He sat down across from me and said, "Brandt Tobler, you are not allowed in any Dillard's anywhere in the country for the rest of your life." He then slid me a piece of paper and told me to sign it. The paper read: Termination. Fired for mail fraud, sending personal letters on company stationery.

I signed it and then just sat there in this weird silence, not sure what was going to happen next. The cop then said, "Okay. Stand up so we can walk you off the property." Right then it hit me. I had done it, I had beaten those fools. I was the Mallfia boss. I was not going to jail. I was free. I was John Gotti! I stood up and walked out of the conference room. They could have walked me out the employee exit that was maybe 50 yards away, but instead, all five of them decided to walk me all the way around the store. I think they thought this would be embarrassing, but it was actually the greatest victory lap of all time.

 We got to the front doors, and I turned around with a huge smile on my face, and said, "Thank you guys so much for allowing me the opportunity to work here." Not one of them said a word, and I turned around and walked out the front doors. I have never been in another Dillard's since that day.

Looking back, I know that I was very lucky to survive. I mean, how many mafia bosses ever get out alive? I was also a little worried that there still could be some repercussions. So, a week after the Mallfia came to an end, I decided I was leaving town. I packed up all my stuff and headed south for Phoenix. Two of my closest friends had moved to Phoenix. They were going to junior college, and working out every day to try out for the basketball team in the spring. I still occasionally had dreams of playing college basketball, and decided this time, I was going to make it happen. I told myself I would work my ass off every day and make the team. Even though I already had a fake/real college degree, I thought I would go back to junior college for the third time, and try to get an actual real degree. I figured, again, that being a P.E. teacher/high school basketball coach was the only job that I would actually enjoy in life. I felt like I had matured and was ready to really start working on my future. I knew I had partied enough. It was time to start acting like an adult.

I arrived in Phoenix in the middle of June, which was a mistake, because it was so damn hot every day. Growing up in Wyoming, 95 degrees was about as hot as it would get, so I wasn't ready for the wall of 118-degree heat the minute I stepped off the airplane. Luckily, I was able to hit the ground running, because my friend Richard had everything set up for me on my arrival. We had grown up in Cheyenne together, and his family had always treated me like one of their own. I was going to live with him at his uncle's house, and he had lined up full-time jobs for us in his uncle's warehouse at the airport. We spent most days sweeping the floor, sorting through junk, and sweating all over a huge airplane hanger and an old office building. It was hard work, but Richard and I always made it fun by turning everything into a competition. Our favorite game was who could throw and break the most junk while also trying to fill up the old green dumpsters fastest. We ate lunch at the same Mexican restaurant every day, and one day, we had a chance encounter. I had no idea the direction of my life would change forever based on the interaction that was about to transpire.

On a scorching Friday afternoon, we walked into the restaurant, and to my amazement, I saw one of my high school friends sitting in the back booth. It was my buddy Matt Farwell, who I hadn't seen in months. He hopped up and gave me a huge hug. Over tacos, Matt asked me what made me move to Phoenix, and I told him that I was there for college, and planned on being a teacher and coach in Wyoming when I finished my degree. That's when Matt became the catalyst propelling me on my life trajectory. All he said was: "That's awesome, but I always thought you'd become a comedian. You were always the funniest kid in school."

At first, I was kind of flattered, but I had never even considered being a comedian. Growing up in Wyoming, there weren't any comedians or a comedy club. In my head, comedians only lived in New York City or Hollywood. But I couldn't get the thought out of head. Later that afternoon, as we were cleaning out an old office, I asked Richard, "Do you really think I could be a comedian?" He said, "Sure, why not?" For the next three weeks, I spent all day thinking and dreaming about being a stand-up comedian. I wanted to do it, but I had no idea where to start.

At my first meeting with my new university's guidance counselor, I asked if I could major in comedy. He laughed: "That's really funny. There is not a stand up comedy major here, but you can sign up for a public speaking class and see if you can make your fellow students laugh." So... I signed up for the class! I ended up loving it. The thrill of being the center of attention, while also occasionally making my fellow classmates laugh immediately made it my favorite class. Growing up, I always got in trouble for getting up in front of the class and being a goofball, but in this class it was encouraged. I was a little nervous before I gave my first speech. The topic? If I were an animal I'd be... I picked a monkey. I told a couple of jokes and performed some monkey act-outs. My speech actually got a couple laughs. I loved the way I felt when I heard the other students laughing. This class was something I looked forward to twice a week, and it made college fun this first time.

Everything in my life was going great, and I loved living in Phoenix. My friends back in Wyoming were stuck in the snow and wind, while I was lying by the pool most days, working on my tan. I made new friends, the nightlife was incredible, and I spent every Sunday with my grandparents, who had moved to Phoenix to get away from the brutal Wyoming winters. They were my favorite people, and they always made sure I had everything I needed. The only thing I missed about Cheyenne was my girlfriend, Vickie. She was a beautiful, smart, funny blonde that I had been dating for just over a year. I was certain I would marry Vickie some day. She was going to school at the University of Wyoming in Laramie and was doing great in her freshmen year. I was so in love with her, and we really worked hard on communicating and making each

other feel like we were a major part of each other's days, even if we were 900 miles away from each other. We would send hand-written letters, surprise packages, emails, and I would get a new calling card every other day so we could talk for hours every night. I felt like leaving Cheyenne was the best decision I had ever made, and my future was looking brighter than ever!

Then one afternoon, everything changed. I came home from school, and my roommate handed me a letter that I just assumed was from Vickie. She sent a letter or package about every three days, and I never got mail from anybody else. Her envelopes were always decorated with hearts and kisses, but this envelope was different. It was plain, except for a big red stamp in the left corner. I glanced at it, and the first two words I saw were Correctional Facility. I immediately dropped that letter on the kitchen table like it was a hot potato. I knew it was from my dad, and I didn't even want to touch it. I couldn't remember the last time I talked to my dad. Everything in my life was going great, so that letter scared the shit out of me. I went to dinner and the gym like I did every night, and when I got home, I walked by the kitchen table without even looking to see if the letter was still there. I was hoping it was gone.

But, as I lay in bed, staring at the ceiling fan, I knew I wasn't going to be able to go to sleep until I opened that letter. I tiptoed to the kitchen so that I wouldn't wake my roommates and saw that the letter was still on the table. I grabbed it and tiptoed back to my room. I locked my bedroom door, sat on the edge of my bed, and opened the envelope very slowly and carefully, as if my dad might pop out. I read the two-page letter three times in a row. My dad gave me an update on his life. He said over and over how much he missed me and my brother and how much he loved us. He said that even though he hasn't talked to us in years, we should never forget that blood is thicker than water. No matter what, he would always be there for us, and he would always be our dad.

It's hard to have somebody tell you that they will always be there for you when you haven't seen them in eight years. He missed my 16th birthday, all of my basketball games, my prom, my high school graduation, and so many other important days. Countless times, I just wished he would have been there to give me a hug and say that he was proud of me, like a lot of my friends' dads did. Despite my feelings, the letter did make me feel good. I cried while I read it, but I also smiled. It was great to hear from him, and it made me feel good to know that he was always thinking about us. After reading the last paragraph of the letter, I knew I wouldn't sleep that night. The last paragraph said that my dad would be at the Phoenix airport in three days and that he would love to see me. He said I shouldn't bother writing back because he wouldn't get it in time. Instead, he would just be looking for me at the airport and was really hoping I would be there. The next morning I didn't tell my roommates or Vickie what the letter said. I just read it over and over the next two days, always alone in my room with the door locked. I didn't know what to do. He had essentially given up on my brother and me for the last eight years, but he was still my dad. I fought with the decision, but as the day got closer, the decision got easier. I was going to go see my dad.

I woke up the morning that he was scheduled to arrive, nervous as a kid on his first day of school. I bought a brand new outfit the day before because I wanted my dad to think I looked cool (not sure why I thought he had any fashion sense after wearing the exact same prison uniform for most of his adult life). I wanted to bring all my trophies, newspaper clippings, and high school diploma to show him everything he missed, but I decided to just bring a picture of my girlfriend and a big picture of me playing basketball (the one that was on the front page of the Cheyenne newspaper). I made it to the airport in record time that day, but when I got there, I realized I had no idea what my own dad looked like. I hadn't seen him for eight years. I didn't know if he had long hair or short hair, if he was fat or skinny, or if he had a big beard or neck tattoos. I didn't even really know how tall he was.

This was pre-9/11, so I just walked around from gate to gate poking my head in bars and bookstores asking myself, is that my dad in the suit? Is that my dad in the polo shirt? It felt like going to a mall and coming out eight years later trying to remember where you parked. You have an idea, but you're not really sure. But of course, when you see your car, you know it's yours.

When I came around the corner and saw a guy in tan khaki pants, a wife-beater, and a ponytail, I immediately knew he was my dad. He looked just like me! I ran over and gave him a huge hug, and we both tried (unsuccessfully) to fight off the tears. He just kept wiping tears from my cheek saying, "I am so happy to see you son. I am so happy you are here!"

He was only there for a layover, which of course he didn't tell me in his letter, so we only had about 50 minutes to catch up. I spent the next 46 minutes talking as fast as I could telling him everything that he missed. The last four minutes, he finally told me how proud he was of me and how much he loved and missed my brother and me. But just like every time when I was young, he was there for a short time of fun and love, and then before I knew it, he was gone. Before he boarded his plane, he told me that his first priority was to be a better father to us and we were both welcome to come visit him anytime at his new home in Las Vegas. Then, he gave me a big hug, told me he loved me one last time, and then walked down the tunnel to his plane. I sat at the window of his gate, and I watched his plane take off

into a beautiful Arizona sunset. I remember seeing my huge smile in the reflection of the window.

I drove home that day feeling for the first time in my life like my dad really was my dad. That night I called Vickie and told her every detail of what happened that day. For the next couple of days, I couldn't stop thinking about our meeting, so I called Casey and Tim back in Cheyenne, and told them everything that happened. Given that we had bonded over how shitty our dads had always been, even joking when we dropped out of LCCC that at least our dads wouldn't have to miss another graduation, they were so excited for me. I told them my dad had said that I could come visit anytime, and that made them excited, because they had never been to Vegas. An hour later, they called me back and said, "Let's go to Las Vegas!"

We decided that they would come to Phoenix to pick me up, and we would head straight there. They were excited to party, and I couldn't wait for them to meet my dad. After all, they had heard so much about him. They left Cheyenne two days later and made the 14-hour drive straight to Phoenix. My bags were already packed when they arrived, but when they got there, they were so tired we ended up staying at my place so they could rest. The next day, we woke up at 7:00 a.m. and immediately hit the road. No showers or breakfast—we wanted to get to Vegas by noon! On the four-hour car ride to Sin City, we listened to the same Eminem tape over and over. At the time, he was just a white dude nobody had really heard of from Detroit.

Eminem also didn't have a father around growing up, so my friends felt a real connection to him. They sang every word about hating your dad with the passion I used to also have. But I didn't have to hate my dad anymore. My dad was back! We got to Vegas, and our first stop was the legendary Stardust Casino to find my dad. When we walked into the casino, I spotted him sitting at a back table, drinking a Jack and Coke, and watching four different basketball games on the big screen TVs. I ran over and gave him a big hug. With a huge smile on his face, he gave my friends hugs. Then he asked, "Are you guys ready to fuck up Vegas?" We all smiled and replied, "YES!" and he said, "Well let's fucking go!" My dad immediately taught us how to bet sports parlays and showed us how to flirt with cocktail waitresses. We couldn't believe we could get drinks for free! We were shocked that all we had to do is give a hot young girl a dollar, and she would keep coming back with cold drinks forever. For the next five days and four nights, he took us up and down the strip where we gambled, drank, puked, drank some more, saw a ton of beautiful women, and laughed until the sun came up each morning. My friends and I instantly fell in love with Las Vegas and agreed that it was the best week of our lives.

Before we loaded our car to head back home, my dad said we were all welcome back anytime. He said if we didn't mind a full house, we could all live with him and his cocktail waitress girlfriend, Tiffany, in her doublewide trailer. We told my dad thanks for the offer, but we had to get back to college. Living in Las Vegas would be so much fun, but we all knew our families would kill us if we dropped out of college again. But the thing was... once that seed had been planted, we couldn't get the idea out of our heads. We talked about living in Vegas the whole drive back to Phoenix and came to a group decision. Who cared what our families thought? We were adults, and we were moving to Las Vegas. It was an easy decision for my friends because Las Vegas is a lot more exciting than Cheyenne, Wyoming. And I loved the idea, because the chance to have a real relationship with my real father was something I never imagined could, or would ever, happen. We decided that we would all drop out of junior college, move to Vegas, and get jobs as pirates at Treasure Island Casino. Treasure Island did this hourly show where two enormous pirate ships fought with big fake explosions and fireworks. The pirates would jump off the ships into the water, and the crowd would go crazy. It seemed like our dream job. Who needs a college degree when you can have a fake sword, wear an eye patch, and have hundreds of cute tourist girls scream for you daily?

My friends dropped me off in Phoenix and headed back to Cheyenne to move out of their apartments and pack up all their stuff. They let everybody back home know that they were done with the cold weather, and if you needed to find them, their new residency would be next to a swimming pool in fabulous Las Vegas, Nevada. A little over three weeks after they dropped me off in Phoenix, they were back to pick me up. We loaded up all of my stuff. We were so excited to be on our way to Sin City to start our new lives! In hindsight, this was an awful decision. I was finally doing great in school, but the temptation of having my dad back in my life was much more important to me then a college degree. Vickie tried to talk me out of it, but in the end, she knew my bags were packed the second my Dad invited us.

Upon arriving in Vegas, we moved all of our stuff into Tiffany's three-bedroom trailer. Tiffany was a very sweet mother of three and was so generous and nice to us the second we got in to town. Her three adult children lived with her, and they were a little shocked when they were told we were moving in just as we parked in their driveway. Regardless, they greeted us with hugs and all volunteered to help us unload our stuff. With our arrival, there were now nine people, three loud-ass birds, and two mini annoying dogs living together in the little trailer. The trailer was more than full, and lived up to every white-trash stereotype you could think of. Tiffany was in her late 40s with great boobs, but you could tell the late Vegas nights had really taken their toll on her. Tiffany's oldest daughter was a very hot stripper in her late 20's, and her middle daughter was in her early 20's and in the military. She was stationed in Alaska but was on leave, and was

only going to be around for a couple of months. Tiffany's youngest was 18, and he and his best friend (who also lived in the trailer) had dropped out of high school, and had no brains and no talent. However, they both thought they were geniuses and Greek gods. Every morning they did a 20-minute workout in the front yard, which they swore was their training program so they could become Navy Seals. Add to that my jobless dad, fresh out of prison, and top it all off with three hicks from Wyoming on a mission to be fake pirates it was definitely the ghetto Brady Bunch.

The only thing we all had in common was we all loved to get drunk... all day and all night. We were a reality show long before they even existed. Us five dudes had to share one bedroom, and in it was just one mattress and a box spring side by side on the floor. If you were one of the first two to go to bed, you got the mattress. The remaining three would fight over the couch. Nobody wanted to sleep on the box spring. These were awful sleeping conditions, but being new to Vegas, we spent very few hours in the trailer, so it wasn't that bad. Most nights, we drank so much we passed out anywhere that was open in the trailer instead of actually trying to find the bed or couch. It was as if we had dropped out of college but somehow moved into a frat house on wheels. My dad and Tiffany would get the drunkest, and they would always fight over the fact that he didn't have a job and was always spending all of her $1 bills. My dad, my two friends, and I would get kicked out of the trailer consistently every three weeks. We would have to pack up all of our stuff and go stay in a weekly hotel with the pimps, hookers, crack heads, low life gangsters, and European tourists who thought they were getting a good hotel deal just off the strip. Those weekly hotels are the last place you would ever want to live. My dad would often say that staying there was worse than prison. He would eventually get back in Tiffany's good graces, and we would get to move back into the trailer, which felt like a mansion after living in those weekly dumps. Unfortunately, this cycle kept going and going, and we would go from trailer to shit hotel for the next couple months.

To make things worse, Treasure Island never called us back about our pirate dream jobs. At that point, Casey and Tim decided to give up on Vegas and head back to Cheyenne, and re-enroll back in school. They were always a lot smarter than me! In hindsight, I definitely should have moved back home with them. I missed my amazing girlfriend and my family, and I just wasn't doing anything productive. I spent most days laying by the pool getting drunk, tan, and fat. But I loved seeing my dad every day, so I decided I couldn't leave. I ended up getting a job emptying slot machines from 11 pm to 8 am, four nights a week, at the Klondike Casino. The reason you have never heard of the Klondike Casino is that it is a complete dump located 12 miles southeast of the Strip. It was full of cigarette smoke, old people, and depression. This was an awful job. The place was a complete shithole, and there is nothing worse than being broke and having to count others people's money all night long. My Mallfia instincts kicked in, and I spent every day trying to figure out how to rob the casino. Unfortunately, the real Mafia had already robbed this casino years ago, so they had much better security than the Cheyenne Dillard's. This job really took the life out of me, and after two months of working there, my spirit was broken. The initial excitement of living in Vegas had worn off, and as much as I loved hanging out with my dad, I was ready to move back to Cheyenne. I didn't have any real friends in Vegas, and I wasn't happy. Just like everybody else, Vegas had officially beaten me. I couldn't take the constant fighting and shitty life at the trailer. Depression was really setting in. I spent everyday dreaming of Cheyenne, my girlfriend, my family, and my friends. I started picking up extra shifts at my miserable job with the intention of making every dollar I could. I was spending as little money as possible, and all my free time was spent at the gym shooting hoops by myself. I told myself as soon as I saved up $1,500, I was moving back to Wyoming.

100 MILES

AND
RUNNING

One day, I walked onto the basketball court at my gym in Vegas and met a guy named Kevin, who would change my life forever. Kevin was a tall charming redhead who everybody in the gym loved… until he lost playing basketball and turned into a huge asshole. He hated to lose, and that is what initially brought us together. I was also super competitive and miserable to be around when I lost. Luckily for me, I got on his team a few times in my first couple of weeks at the gym, and we kept winning and winning, so we quickly became friends. One day I asked him what he did for a living, and he said he was a professional gambler. "Like a card counter?" I asked, and he said, "No, we bet on sports every day." I was in awe.

"That has to be the best job in the world!" I told him (Even better than being a fake pirate, I thought).

He just chuckled and replied, "It's a pretty good job most days, but there are a lot of ups and downs."

I had so many more questions, but I could tell he was in no hurry to be interviewed by a starry-eyed kid. I was now fascinated by Kevin and started asking other guys in the gym about him. I found out that most of the guys that played in the lunch game were professional gamblers, but they all said Kevin was by far the most successful. They told me Kevin was a multi-millionaire. I was in shock and couldn't believe I had a friend that was a millionaire. The richest guy I knew in growing up in Cheyenne had maybe $50,000, so this was big for me. Every few days, I would ask Kevin what games I should bet, and he would always say, "Don't bet kid, you can't beat these casinos." But I was persistent, because I knew if he just told me which teams he was betting, I could become a millionaire. I started waiting for him in the parking lot, making sure we walked into the gym together, which would usually guarantee that we would be on the same team. Over the next couple months, I kept getting on his team, and I would always play my ass off to ensure that we would win our games. The more we won, the closer we got, and every couple of days I would say to him, "Come on man, just give me one game to bet." After pestering him for weeks, he finally caved in and told me to follow him into the dark hallway behind the basketball court.

When we got back there, he looked around to make sure nobody was around or could hear him, and when he felt safe, he said, "Alright kid, I will tell you the four big games we are betting this weekend. Promise me you won't tell anybody else in the gym what we are betting. These games are secret, and I don't want them to know what we are doing." I promised him I wouldn't tell anybody. I was shocked he actually told me, and I was so excited because I knew these four games were going to change my life. I drove home from the gym as fast as I could that day, and immediately told my dad that my new friend the-millionaire-professional-gambler gave me his secret games. At the time, I had saved up $800 dollars, and if I bet it all on a four team parlay, when these four secret games won I would have over $9,600.

Side note: If you don't know how a parlay works, it's when you bet a group of games, and if they all win, you hit a big payout, but all four have to win. If three win and one loses, you still lose all your money. For example, if I bet four games and they all win, I get back 11 times what I bet. So if I bet $800, I get back my $800, plus another $8800, for a total of $9600. If you bet five games, it's 22 times what you bet, six games payout at 45 times what you bet, seven games are 100 times what you bet, and so on, all the way up to 15 games. A parlay is a common bet by degenerate gamblers, because it is a way to take a little money and turn it into a lot.

My only thought was, when these four games won, I would easily reach my goal of $1,500. I could move home, be with my girlfriend, and most importantly, never have to work at that shitty Klondike Casino again. I went to the closest Wells Fargo bank and pulled out every dollar I had. The bank teller asked me, "Mr. Tobler, is everything alright? Do you want to close your account?" "No way!" I replied. "Don't worry, I will be back on Monday with a lot more money than this." My dad convinced Tiffany to give him $2,500 and promised to give her the money back, with interest, on Monday, and take her on a beautiful vacation to Napa Valley with his winnings. He was going to bet that $2,500, plus the little money he had saved on his own, so when all four games won, he would get back over $30,000. We literally bet all the money we could get our hands on, even our change, on these four games. They were secret games from a millionaire – they couldn't lose! Now, I am sure I don't need to tell you what happened next.

Vegas
+ My Dad's Luck
We're Screwed

We lost the very first game, which meant it didn't matter what happened in the other three games. Our ticket was a loser, and my dad and I had lost all of our money. All four of the games lost that day and I remember thinking, man, I wish that dumb fucking redhead at my gym would have kept his secret games a secret from me! I was crushed, broke, and I had gotten my dad in big trouble. Now I had to start all over. I couldn't move back to Cheyenne, because I had no money. To make things worse, my dad's girlfriend wanted to kick us out of her trailer again, but we had lost every dollar we had, so we had nowhere to go. We made a deal with her that we would help around the house more, I would ask for overtime at work, and my dad would get a job. My dad started cleaning carpets, and I spent every hour at the casino. I was still miserable counting money all night, but now the general manager let me vacuum the whole casino each morning to give me a couple extra hours of work each week.

I promised myself that I would save all my money and when I got to $1,500, I would move home no matter what. As much as I hated the thought of going back to junior college for the fourth time, I realized I had nothing really going on in my life, and I needed to get my shit together. I was going to work hard, become a great teacher and head basketball coach, and help our youth. The worst part of losing all of my money was that I couldn't go to the gym and play basketball anymore. For my entire life, basketball had been my stress reliever, and shooting hoops always cheered me up when I was having a bad day. Now, every free hour I had was spent at work, and I didn't have any extra gas money to go anywhere on the rare occasions that I wasn't at work.

After a month of hard work, I finally saved up a little extra spending money and I was able to go back to the gym. Kevin was on the phone when I walked in, but he immediately ended his phone call when we made eye contact. I sat down by myself on a bench at the far end of the gym and began to lace up my shoes. Kevin came over and sat down right next to me and looked very concerned.

"Where have you been?"

"I've been working."

He then put his hand on my shoulder and said, "I have been thinking about you a lot, kid. Please tell me you didn't bet those games I gave you."

"Unfortunately I bet every single one of them with every dollar I had."

He just shook his head, and laughed. "I'm sorry kid, but I tried to tell you not to bet. If it makes you feel any better we lost around $850,000 that day."

Yeah, that is a lot of money, but honestly, it didn't make me feel any better. I didn't care how much money he lost, because I knew he didn't lose all of his money like I did. He then asked, "Can you come to lunch with us today? I am buying, and I got an idea for me and you that I think might work."

Of course, I said yes. If anybody could have used a free lunch at the time, it was me. But I was in no hurry to hear his idea, since his last secret brilliant idea made me lose every dollar I had. When we got to the sandwich shop, there were eight guys from the gym standing around the counter ordering, and after everybody had ordered, Kevin pulled out a giant wad of one hundred dollar bills and paid for everybody's lunch. We then sat at the very back table, and he began asking me question after question while I ate my delicious free sandwich. He wanted to know about my life growing up and how I ended up in Vegas. He was very interested in exactly why I moved to Vegas and how I ended up at that gym. Looking back, I now realize it was a job interview.

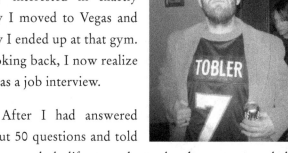

After I had answered about 50 questions and told him my whole life story, he took a long pause and then asked, "Do you want to work for me?"

"I don't know, I already have a job and right now my only goal is to save up $1,500 and move back to Wyoming. I really miss my girlfriend and family, so I probably will only be here a couple more months."

He just chuckled, shook his head, and said, "The job you have sucks and you can move back whenever you want. But from now on you work for me."

I looked at him with a blank stare, because I was so confused. How could I work for him when I didn't even know what the job was? He didn't tell me what I would be doing, how much it paid, or even when and where I worked. I assumed he could see my confusion because he just stood up, placed his hand on my head, and said, "Trust me, kid, you want this job. Let's go." Everybody else stood up and followed him outside. I had always noticed at the gym that he was the leader of the crew. When he did something everybody else just got in line and followed his move. When we got outside, everybody headed for their cars, and as I walked towards my own, Kevin asked me, "What are you doing the rest of the day?" I told him I had no plans, and he said, "Good, you will go with Anthony then." And just like that, I was hired and immediately started working what would end up being the greatest, craziest job in the world.

Anthony was a 6'4" ex-MLB player who was, by far, the best athlete and most-liked guy at our gym. He was handsome, charming, and had a way of making everybody he spoke with feel special. He was my first friend at the gym and always the guy I wanted to sit and talk to when we weren't playing. Kevin always tried to set it up so the three of us were on the same team, because then it didn't matter who our other two players were, we could not be beat. Anthony was Kevin's right hand man, and they were always together. When Kevin said I should go with Anthony, I was a little scared, but he instantly made me feel safe when he said, "Come on little fella, let's get to work," as we both climbed into his brand new black BMW. Again, this was a big deal for me, because as a Wyoming kid, I had never been in a BMW in my life. I thought it was so cool riding shotgun in such a nice car.

We had a 20-minute drive down to the strip, and that was just enough time for me to ask Anthony a thousand questions about my new job. Anthony explained to me that I had just been hired to be a "runner." Here is how the job works. My bosses worked in an office a few miles off the strip and were constantly getting information about games from all over the country. They would then use that information to bet offshore, mainly over the phones. There really weren't any internet betting websites at the time. Instead, you would call a 1-800 number, give them a code name and password, and ask what their spread was on a game. If the spread was the number you wanted, then you would bet it. If the spread wasn't the number you wanted, you would just say pass and hang up. As I mentioned, this was before the internet became what is it today, so if somebody got arrested, suspended, hurt, the weather changed, or any other circumstance arose that would give us an advantage, we most likely knew that info 10 to 20 minutes before the casinos and offshore places did. There were a lot of other professional gamblers around America at the time, so you wanted to get the information before them and then get your bet in before they did. How good the information was made a difference on how much the line would move. For example, if the Broncos are playing the Raiders and the spread on the game is Broncos -3, but you find out the Raiders quarterback got arrested (which is always a possibility), you want to bet the Broncos -3 before the world finds out that the Raiders quarterback is out. That is because when that information comes out publicly, the spread on the game will be something close to Broncos -7.

You want to be laying -3 when the rest of the world is laying -7. This gives you a huge advantage. If you don't understand the sports analogy, another way to explain it would be think about the stock market. Let's say Apple stock is selling for 45 dollars, but you find out that they are secretly releasing the new iPhone tomorrow, so you want to get the $45 stock now, because tomorrow it will probably be a $75 stock. Obviously, you have quite the advantage when you are buying stock at $30 less than the rest of the world.

Our job as "runners" was to run up and down the strip and bet the games before other runners bet the games, and the casinos changed the odds. We had walkie-talkies, and when we were supposed to bet something, my boss would yell it over the walkie-talkie and we would try to beat the other runners to make sure we bet the game first. If you were first, you got to bet the game at -3 before it moved to -4 or -5. At the time, there were a lot of runners on the streets, and it was very competitive. Anthony gave me a pretty good description of the job, and I had a rough idea of what I would be doing. Before I knew it, we pulled up to the Bally's Casino valet and Anthony looked at me.

"You ready?"

"I think so."

"Good" he said, "because it's go-time." He then handed me $22,000 and said, "Go in and bet this on Duke football +34."

I was shocked. "Duke is awful! They are going to get killed. They haven't won a football game in like two years."

"Let me tell you the most important rule in this job: you never question anything. Sometimes it might not make sense, but there is a reason why we do everything. Just always do exactly what you are told." Anthony said stoically.

So, I walked into Bally's with $11,000 in each front pocket of my shorts. I approached the counter with sweaty palms and shaky hands and I said, "I would like to bet Duke +34 for $22,000." The ticket writer looked at me in shock and called the supervisor over. The supervisor asked, "How much do you want?" I mumbled, "twenty-two thousand" and he said okay. I handed them the money and they counted it right there in front of me. It was crazy to think all of that money was just in my pockets. When the ticket writer got to the last hundred-dollar bill in the stack, he said, "Okay we are right. Here you go." He handed me a ticket that read Duke +34 for $22,000 to win $42,000. I walked out the front doors of the casino holding that ticket as tight as I could. I was guarding it like it was my firstborn child.

Anthony trained me every day for the next three weeks. He took me to each casino and showed me where to park so I could get in and out easy and safe. He also introduced me to the people I should talk to and who to avoid in each sports book. He taught me every trick he had learned in his five years on the job. On the first day of my fourth week, he told me to meet him for lunch so we could go over some things. I drove to a little sandwich spot, Capriotti's, which we both loved. When I walked in, Anthony was sitting at the back table all by himself. I walked to the back and he gave a big hug and said, "Have a seat. You can order in a minute." There was a brown paper sack sitting in the middle of the table and, assuming it was food, I asked him if he already ordered and whether I should get my food to go. He said, "Open it up." When I did, all I saw were hundred dollar bills in small stacks, bundled up with rubber bands. Anthony said, "That's yours. There's $150,000 cash in there, and it's your bankroll. You are responsible for that money 24 hours a day, 7 days a week, 365 days a year."

Over the next couple of months, this bankroll would get as high as $450,000 and as low as $60,000. When we would win, and the bankroll got over $300,000, I would give my bosses a bunch of money. When we would lose, and it got under $100,000, they would give me more money. Overall I always had somewhere around $150,000 with me at all times. I would try to keep most of the money in winning tickets or casino chips, but I always needed at least $50,000 in cash so I could run in and make a bet at any casino, at any time. Given that the whole goal of the job was to beat the other runners out on the streets and

to always get my bosses the best numbers, I had to be on call all hours of the day and night. There were countless Thursday and Friday nights that I was sneaking around betting college football games at 10 or 11 p.m. when none of the other runners were on the streets. The craziest part was that each night, I would bring home around $150,000 to the $90,000 trailer we lived in. I loved to play with the cash, just like I used to do with my Halloween candy when I was a kid. I would spell my name with stacks of hundreds, build pyramids, and just lay on piles of it and smile. Cash is my favorite toy and playing with it never ever gets old (and yes, I know it's filthy).

The job was going great, but the first problem we had was with Kevin's partner Oliver. Kevin had hired me while Oliver was back home in Kentucky for a month helping out with his family. When Oliver came back to Vegas, he was very suspicious. He didn't understand how a broke kid from Wyoming with this sappy story about his father just showed up at Kevin's very expensive gym, and was suddenly working for him. He thought I was a plant from the FBI. He was very cautious, because he had been busted before and was almost sentenced to prison for a long time. I don't need to go into a lot of the details, but let's just say by some crazy coincidence, a guy got murdered in a phone booth and there was no case without the state's star witness. I am sure it was just a little mix-up over who was next to use the phone.

The first month of work, I spent every free moment with Kevin and Oliver. Kevin told Oliver that he trusted me, and that he had asked me a thousand questions and everything checked out. It still didn't make sense to Oliver, so he decided to interrogate me every time he saw me. "So you dropped out of school and moved here to be a pirate?" I could feel him watching my every move for those first two weeks, but after a while, he realized I was too dumb to work for the FBI and he let his guard down. From then on, he didn't treat me like an employee, but rather a close friend.

I really did work for the two coolest bosses in the world. Most days I would wake up, play basketball for two hours, go eat a free lunch, head to the strip and bet from 3pm-7pm, and then go out to a free dinner at a nice restaurant, where we would spend all night drinking beers and watching all the games we bet that day. For a kid who loves sports, beer, and crab legs, every day was like a dream come true. I couldn't have been happier. Kevin and Anthony were like the dad and big brother I always wanted. I was spending very little time at the trailer and most of my time at Kevin's incredible 10,000 square foot mansion. We spent every Sunday night in Kevin's backyard swimming, barbecuing, and hanging out with his kids. I think my dad was happy for me, but also a little jealous. Back in his drug dealing days, he was the big shot with the pockets full of cash that would come to town, and buy my brother and me whatever we wanted. Now, he saw me idolizing Kevin and we were doing all of these fun things, while he was a carpet cleaner living in a trailer.

Speaking of the trailer, I just couldn't do it anymore. I was making a lot of money, so I decided I was going to rent us a house on the golf course about a half a mile from the trailer. My dad would live there with me and he could still go visit his girlfriend whenever he wanted. Unfortunately, around this time my girlfriend Vickie ended up breaking up with me. She knew when I signed a two-year lease for a beautiful four-bedroom house that I was never coming back. We were going in different directions, and it was obvious that we had started to grow apart. We both knew it was for the best.

Now, all of my focus was on my little brother. I had been calling him daily, and telling him he should move out to Las Vegas and live with us. We could make up for all the lost father-son time we missed out on when we were kids. I promised him we could finally become a happy little family. At the time, my brother was very happy living in Portland. He had a great girlfriend and was enjoying being the manager and most valuable sandwich artist at his neighborhood Subway. But after a month of begging him to move to Vegas, the idea of living happily with his older brother and dad was just too hard to resist. I bought him a one-way ticket and he was on his way! My brother arrived in Vegas and immediately loved it. I called in a favor and got him a job at a stuffed animal store in Caesar's Palace, and he was making new friends daily. He couldn't believe all of the concerts and nightlife that Vegas had to offer. At least once a week, he would come home and tell me he was so happy. The next six months were some of the best days and nights of my life. At least three times a week, my dad, brother, and I would come home from work and sit on the back porch to watch the sun go down while we told stories and drank beer. We would tell him about all the stuff he missed from our childhood, and he would tell us his crazy prison stories. Obviously, his prison yard race-wars were a lot more interesting than my 12-point varsity basketball game stories.

I did tell one story that scared the shit out of my dad. When I was 19 years old, I had sex with a random girl I met at the bowling alley and I got an STD. I was really terrified and didn't want to tell my mom. This was a day I could have definitely used my dad's guidance. My friends all told me if you get an STD you have to go to the doctor and they stick a whole q-tip down the small hole in the tip of your penis that you urinate out of. That sounded so painful, and I knew my favorite body part did not want to go through that, so I asked my friends what else I could do. I decided I had to ask the person that taught me everything I know about sex, and that was my 8th-grade sex ed teacher. He was still a close friend and he said that if I could get my hands on some penicillin that should clear it all up. Luckily, one of my closest friends had just happened to get her wisdom teeth pulled that week, and she had a small bottle of penicillin. I told her everything that happened, and she was more than happy to give me three of her pills. I took all three pills with a big swig of Cherry Coke, and four days later my penis was as good as new.

I thought this story would make my dad laugh, but about half way through it, his face turned white and he looked liked he had seen a ghost. When I finished the story, my dad was speechless and I asked him if he was okay. He said, "Yes, son, I am fine. But that is a scary story because I am deathly allergic to penicillin and I almost died when you were three years old. My doctor prescribed me some penicillin when I was sick, and not knowing I was allergic to it, I took it and almost died in our basement." I just laughed, and said, "Don't worry I am definitely not allergic to it. I have, unfortunately, had to take it a couple times. I think the real problem is I am allergic to condoms and attracted to whores!" That made him laugh, which

also made him relax, and for the next two hours, he told my brother and me his own stories. He must have had sex with more than 75 strippers. He always said young blonde strippers were his kryptonite.

Those patio parties were full of a lot of laughter, hundreds of Coors Lights, and plenty of "I love you sons!" My favorite part of those days were at the end of the night when we would all give each other a big hug, say goodnight, and head to our separate bedrooms. It was so cool to me that we were all living in the same house, and it was our house! My dad, brother and I were finally a happy family. It seemed too good to be true, and of course it was.

Everything was about to change, and it was about to change fast. My dad, brother, and I were counting down the days till he got off parole. To my brother and me, it represented the end of our Dad's past life as a criminal and absentee father. My dad had been waiting for this day for years. He hated going downtown to take weekly piss tests and to meet with his condescending old parole officer. He swore she was the biggest bitch in the world. He would always say, "When I get off parole, I will no longer be controlled by them. I will finally be my own man again." It was a huge day for my dad, and I will never forget the smile on his face the morning of his last day. He had a real bounce in his step, and my brother and I were so excited for him. He said he was going to accomplish some big things, and I believed him.

The night he got off parole, we had a big party and all of our family and his friends came over, and we celebrated this huge accomplishment. Before our family and friends arrived, my brother and I were sitting in the kitchen telling him that we were so proud of him and that he was the best dad in the world. I remember my dad crying and smiling at the same time and repeating, "I did it! I did it! It's finally over, I did it!" That, of course, made my brother and me cry uncontrollably. These were tears of joy for all three of us, and this was a first for us as a family. Our tears usually came with pain. That night we all sang, danced, drank, hugged, and had so much fun. The party raged until the sun came up, and as I stumbled to my bedroom, I had two thoughts. Number one, damn this house is a total disaster and it is going to suck to clean up in the morning. Number 2, I love my dad so much and I am so happy I moved to Las Vegas. At that moment I felt like it was the best decision I had ever made. That night is the last good memory I have of my dad.

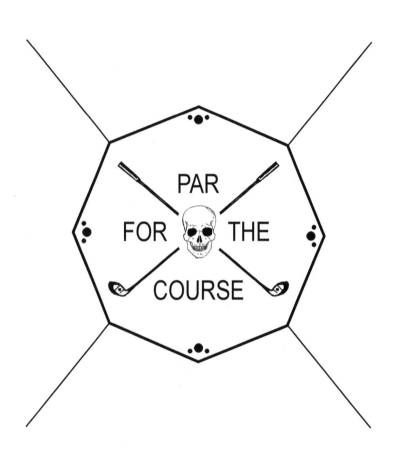

n the days following the party, my dad started bringing around these young white trash kids who were trying so hard to be thugs. Except, they were failing miserably. They tried to pretend like they were gang members, but nobody believed that for a second. They were just young kids hooked on meth that were about the same age as my brother and me. We immediately knew something was wrong, because there is no reason for a man in his late 40s to be hanging out with a bunch of 20 year olds that weren't his kids. He was obviously back on drugs. He acted nothing like the man he had been for the last two years. The house morale, which had been great a week prior, was now getting worse by the second. There were no more "I love you's" or family dinners. Now, it felt like our dad was some punk teenager. He was sneaking around, lying, hiding stuff, always locking his door, and not really having any interaction with us. I hated it, and I was now spending little to no time at the house. Being in that house just made me feel like shit. I was spending all my time at Kevin's house with his wife and three sons. Kevin's house was safe, and I was always so happy when I was with there with his family.

As time went on, my dad got crazier and crazier. I assume the drug use got more rampant, because the number of weird people coming and going from our house at all hours of the night got greater and more frequent each day. At one point, a bunch of my childhood friends from Wyoming visited and somebody stole one of their wallets. I had a feeling it was my dad who did it, so I broke into his bedroom when he was gone and, of course, found the wallet hidden under his bathroom sink. I never thought I would have to tell one of my friends, "Hey man, I am really sorry my dad stole your wallet." That's just something a son should never have to say. It was very embarrassing. Things were starting to get bad, and I knew I had to get my dad out of the house before a disaster happened. Unfortunately, I didn't get him out in time.

Our father-son relationship had come so far in the last two years, but it only took one night to end my relationship with my dad forever. It was a college football Saturday in late September, and it ended up being the final devastating blow to the worst birthday week of my life. Four days earlier, we celebrated my 23rd birthday and, just like the old days, my dad had forgotten all about it. The whole day I was having flashbacks to being a kid again, and the disappointment I felt when he never showed up at my birthday parties. I kept thinking about my 12th birthday party. I had wished my dad would walk through the front doors of Roller City, the roller skating rink where I was having my party, right before I blew out my 12 candles.

I took one last look at the doors and then I blew those candles out as hard as I could. I knew no matter how much I wished he wasn't coming through those doors. Back then, other family members would make excuses for him and I would even tell myself, "Hey, your dad is very busy and if he could be here he would." But as an adult living in the same house as him, I assumed he had to acknowledge it was my big day. I walked by him four or five times that morning, and each time, I was thinking.... this will be the time he says, "Happy Birthday, Son. I love you," but he never said it. And what hurt the most is I know he knew it was my birthday, because he and his drug addict friends ate half of my leftover birthday cake at 5 a.m. the next day.

This crushed me, and I ended up staying at Kevin's house the next couple nights, because seeing him made me sad and furious. On Saturday morning, I left Kevin's house around 6:30 and had to be down at the Strip ready to work by 7. Saturdays were the longest and hardest days of work. I would be running from casino to casino, betting all the football games and halftimes from 7:30 am until 8 pm. These days were exhausting, and I would always come home and try to get to bed early. I had to be up early the next morning to do the exact same thing for the Sunday NFL games. I came home that night and ran into my dad in the kitchen. I noticed his eyes were huge, and he was talking fast and grinding his teeth. I knew he was definitely high on something, but I didn't want to deal with it. I was tired and I had no time to lecture my own dad, so

I just told him, "Dad, I am going to bed and I will be working all day tomorrow. If you want to come down and watch football for a little bit, I can get you a complimentary VIP booth with free lunch and drinks." My dad replied, "Okay, cool." I knew in that moment he was never going to come down to the strip and hang out with me. At this point, it was obvious he didn't want beers and buffets, he only wanted drugs. I walked upstairs to my room, got undressed, and slid into bed. I was too tired to be mad or annoyed with him, I just wanted to go to sleep.

I had only been asleep a couple of hours when my brother burst into my room and woke me up. I was really confused, because I was still half asleep, but I could see by the despair in his face that he was very upset. I asked him what happened, and he just kept saying over and over, "My money is gone! All of my money is gone." He had saved up a little over $350 dollars that he was going to use to fly back to Portland to see his girlfriend graduate from college. When I realized what had happened, I jumped out of bed and ran downstairs to find my dad. I was sure one of his little deadbeat druggie wannabe gangster friends had stolen my little brother's money. When I got downstairs, I yelled and yelled for my dad, but he was nowhere to be found. I went and looked in the garage where he always parked his car, and it was gone. I was standing in the garage telling my brother, "Don't worry, we will get your money back," and then it hit me, "OH SHIT! I have all my work money in my room."

I ran upstairs and dove under my bed to check on the shoebox where I put my money each night. The shoebox was there, so I felt an immediate relief, but then I opened the box and saw my tickets and chips, but no cash. My dad had taken just over $80,000 cash from me while I was sleeping. I fell to the ground and started punching the floor, crying uncontrollably. What was I going to do? I couldn't go tell my bosses that I didn't have $80,000 of their money. My little brother came over and hugged me and kept saying over and over, "I hate him, I hate him, I hate him." He was also crying. In that moment my big brother instincts kicked in. I pulled myself together, hugged him back, and told him, "Don't worry, Ry, it will be okay. I promise it will be okay." We sat on the floor in my bedroom for the next couple hours trying to figure out how and why this happened. We were on an emotional roller coaster that kept going from angry, to sad, to scared, and then back to fucking furious. What made me the most mad was that not only did my dad steal the $80,000 that he knew was my boss's money, but then he had the balls to go into my little brother's room and steal $350 from his own son. The money he watched my brother go to work everyday for, the money he knew my brother was saving for his special trip back to surprise his girlfriend on her big day. I couldn't understand why $80,000 wasn't enough. Did he really need to go take that additional $350 from his youngest son? My dad had broken our hearts again. As we sat there crying, I decided this was going to be the last time he made my brother and me cry.

It also started to set in that I had a huge problem, because I didn't know what I was going to tell Kevin. He was my hero, and he was the one person in life I didn't want to disappoint. I stayed up all night crying and trying to figure out the best way to say, "Hey boss, we have a tiny little problem, I am $80,000 short." I had a little hope that I would be able to get the money back, but I knew I had to buy myself some time. My brother and I waited all night for my dad to come back home, but he never did. I decided to call Kevin early Sunday morning and tell him that I couldn't work because I had food poisoning and had been throwing up all night. He wasn't happy, because an NFL Sunday was a huge day for us, but he said, "Hope you feel better, and if you do, go work the afternoon games" and hung up. Sundays are so busy in the office that he had no time to talk. I knew I had to try to find my dad before he blew all the money. My brother and I got in my car and drove to all the bars and sports books we knew he usually frequented. He was nowhere to be found. After driving around for almost seven hours, we decided to call off the search and head home. We were exhausted and emotionally drained.

My dad finally showed back up at the house that night around 9 pm, and he was the highest I had ever seen him. The second we heard the garage door opening, my brother and I ran downstairs and confronted him as he got out of his car. We both were screaming at him, asking him over and over where our fucking money was, and how could he have done that to us? He denied taking the money, while yelling back at us that we were ungrateful, irresponsible pieces of shit that probably got drunk and lost our money. The more we yelled at him, the more hateful and hurtful he got. He began saying awful things about us, and then about our mom and grandparents. The final straw was when he got about an inch away from Ryan's face, and screamed, "I don't think I am even your dad! Your whore mother was fucking every railroader in town." I saw my brother's face just drop, and he was done yelling. He just started crying. I grabbed my brother by the arm and said, "Let's go." We walked out of that house both crying again. We got in my car and I slammed the driver's side door as hard as I could. My dad followed us outside and stood at the top of the driveway, still screaming the meanest things he could think of.

As I sped off, I only had one thought in my head. I am going to kill that motherfucker! That's it, I don't ever want to see him again. He can't keep doing this to us. I have to kill

this motherfucker. Now, I am no killer, and I really didn't learn how to murder people in my failed years at junior college. But I did remember his reaction when I told him the story about the time I got an STD. I remembered his story about how he almost died from an allergic reaction to penicillin. My dad was a notorious liar, so I decided to call my mom and ask her if that story was true. She verified his story and asked if everything was okay. My dad had put my mom through so much already, and I knew if I told her what he had just done to us, it would crush her. I had my answer. Penicillin was now my new best friend. My life had now become a real-life version of the board game Clue. I knew what the murder weapon would be, I just didn't know what room it would happen in, and who the killer would be. When I hung up the phone with my mom, my only thought was where could I get some penicillin.

Your first murder is always the hardest! Like I said earlier, I am not a killer, but lucky for me, I knew one. And he just happened to be the most loyal person in my life. My cousin was a real gangster who was known on the streets as KILLA KADO! At one point, he was the youngest

person to ever go to the Wyoming State Penitentiary, and if I had to describe him in one word, it would be fearless. Obviously, I can't give his resume out in public, but I will tell you this: he is not to be messed with, because he does not negotiate. In his defense, he is also the sweetest guy I know. I would say he is like a cute kangaroo with an AK-47 hidden in his pouch. I called him and told him everything that had happened. He never liked my dad and always told me that I shouldn't trust him, but he was shocked that he would stoop this low. He agreed that enough was enough and that something had to be done. He said we didn't need to talk about it over the phone anymore, but he would be in Vegas soon. Kado lived in Phoenix, which was a 5-hour drive from Vegas. He must have hung up the phone, packed a bag, and immediately hit the road, because five hours after I hung up, there was a loud knock at the front door. I looked out the peephole not expecting it to be him, but in the shadows of the porch light, there stood my killer. Kado stood silent, with a small bag in his right hand, and a look on his face that I can only describe as angrily focused. I opened the door, and he came in and gave my brother and me huge hugs and immediately asked, "Where's he at?" I instructed him to just sit down and relax for a minute. I then told Kado, "We are going to get him, but I think I have an idea that will keep us out of trouble." So we grabbed a couple beers and went to the back porch to discuss my plan.

Now, before you hear my plan, you have to remember I was only 23 years old, and I had never murdered anybody. This was long before shows like Dexter and Breaking Bad made murdering the bad guys look easy. My plan went like this...first thing we had to do was get some penicillin. Kado said that would be no problem. He said it would take one phone call, and he could probably get it by the end of the day. I don't know how Kado does it, but he always just knows a guy that can get you anything you need. And it doesn't matter which city he is in. I call him my ghetto concierge. I really think he could get me a baby unicorn or a meeting with the President if I just gave him six hours. Before my dad got back on drugs, every day he would go to the Jamba Juice just blocks from our house and get a large Mango-a-Go-Go smoothie. So I figured we would just buy a large smoothie, and fill it up with penicillin. Give the magical smoothie to my dad. My dad would drink it... and then die. My plan was that simple.

I figured there would be no way that he would think we were poisoning his smoothie. I remember Kado just chuckled and said he thought that plan was "cute." He said, "Why don't we just tie him up and jam the pills right down his fucking throat?" I agreed with him that his plan would also work, but as much as I wanted my dad dead, I really didn't want any of us to get in trouble. He conceded that we would try it my way, and if that didn't work, we would do it his way. I figured I would be considered the main suspect if something happened to my dad, so I didn't want to be in the state when it all went down. I was going to fly to Estes Park, Colorado to meet my new girlfriend. On the Jamba Juice day, my brother would load all of his stuff into Kado's car and then get everything ready to execute our plan. They would get the Jamba Juice, fill it up with penicillin, keep it cold in the freezer, and then give it to my dad when he came home. As soon as my dad started drinking it, my brother and cousin would sneak out the back door to Kado's car and drive straight to Phoenix. Then days later, somebody would find my dad laying dead in the house. We would all be out of town, so we could not get blamed. In hindsight, this was an awful plan, but at the time, it seemed flawless.

The Jamba Juice day finally came, so I phoned Kado and my brother from my hotel room in Colorado, and they told me everything was ready to go. They said they had purchased a large peach and mango Jamba Juice, filled it with penicillin, mixed it up really well, put it in the freezer and they were just waiting for my dad to come home. I remember finishing our conversation saying, "Let's get rid of this mother fucker forever... I love you guys." Kado replied, "We love you too," and hung up the phone.

My dad came home, and my brother gave him the
Jamba Juice. He was very annoyed and didn't even think
about drinking it. He sat it on the kitchen table and said,
"I don't want this shit", and then he saw Kado sitting in
the living room and asked my brother, "What the fuck is
he doing here?" He didn't even wait for my brother to
answer, he just kept walking and went up to his room and
locked his door. I don't think my dad thought we were
trying to kill him, but when you know somebody hates
your guts, and they give you a free drink out of nowhere,
you are probably going to be a little skeptical. They put the
Jamba Juice back in the fridge and waited for him to come
back downstairs. They were hoping that he was getting
high in his room, would forget they gave it to him, see it in
the fridge, and drink it. About an hour later, he came back

downstairs, but he walked right by my brother and cousin without saying a word. He walked right by the fridge, out the kitchen door to his car in the garage, and drove off.

The second my dad drove away, Kado called to tell me that they had given my dad the drink, but he had ignored it. "Shit," I said, "well, I guess you guys should just stick with the rest of the plan and head for Phoenix. I will be back in Vegas in three days, I will move everything out of the house, and we will try to avoid him for the rest of our lives."

"No. I got a better idea." Kado said. "Now we do it my way. I didn't come all the way up here for this motherfucker to not pay for what he did to you guys. He just left, but when he gets back, Ryan and I are going to get this shit done!"

I, of course, had a million questions, but before I could even get one out, Kado said, "We will call you when this shit is over." Dial tone.

Ryan and Kado opened the garage door. They cut the phone and power lines located in the backyard. Then, they built a hiding spot in the darkest corner of the garage, and they waited. They waited almost two hours for my dad to come home. My dad had this piece of shit Camaro that he thought was the coolest car in the world, and he always made a huge deal about it being parked in the garage. If anybody was ever parked in the driveway, he would come in and make them move their car immediately. His precious Camaro had to be parked safely in the garage, where nothing could possibly happen to it.

My dad finally came home and slowly pulled into the garage, so that the tennis ball he had hung from the ceiling softly bounced upon his windshield. He put the car in park, and repeatedly hit the garage door button located directly above him on his visor. Kado said he got very frustrated and confused, because he didn't understand why the door wasn't shutting behind him. He exited the car and walked over to shut the garage himself. He reached up and manually pulled the garage door down and shut it, locking the door from the inside. The second the door locked and my dad started

walking towards the house, my brother and Kado jumped
out of the dark shadows and tried to beat the shit out of
him with golf clubs. They said they both hit him with a
couple good shots, but it was hard to really get him because
it was so dark. There was only a little light coming in from
a doggie door. My dad went into survival mode. He put his
shoulder down, ran through the locked side door, and fell
into the back yard. Kado chased him into the backyard, but
my dad was able to jump the back wall and run onto the
dark golf course and into the night. He survived, but barely.
There was blood all over the garage floor and all over his
precious, stupid, fucking Camaro.

I think part of what saved him was my brother and
Kado used the wrong clubs. They used a putter and sand

wedge, when they obviously should have used the driver and a 3-wood. I don't know much about murder golf, but it seems like they needed a better caddie. My dad had been in some huge fights when he was in maximum-security prison in Leavenworth, but I would like to think the toughest fight he has ever had was the night he became a driving range in a two-car garage.

I flew back to Las Vegas two days later, and Kado and my brother were long gone. I was nervous coming back to the house. As I entered my neighborhood, I saw the garage door wide open, and my dad's car was not parked in its usual spot. I did a quick walk through the house to see if there was any sign of him, but it looked like my dad had come back to get his Camaro and that was about it. He had left pretty much everything else he owned in his room, and that master bedroom was trashed. I put all of his belongings in six trash bags and threw them in the dumpster.

My dad had left the framed picture of him, my brother, and me that we had given him on Father's Day. I took that picture out of the frame and ripped it into pieces. At that moment, I realized my dream of a father/son relationship was over forever. As far as I was concerned, he was no longer my dad. He was just David Tobler, and I made up my mind I would NEVER speak to David Tobler again. David must have said, "blood is thicker than water" to my brother and me a thousand times in our lives. And as I stood in that garage, holding a garden hose and spraying the floor, trying to clean up the crime scene, I realized that he was right. His blood was much thicker than water. I boxed up all of my stuff, loaded up my car, and headed to a cheap motel on the other side of town. I wanted to get as far away from that house as possible. When I drove away from the house for the last time, tears started to roll down my face. Not because I was going to miss my dad, but because I knew I had to deal with Kevin.

When my dad robbed us that Sunday morning, I told Kevin I had gotten sick and I couldn't work, and I didn't hear from him the rest of the day. The next morning, I woke up and called him early, knowing he wouldn't be up and I would get his voicemail. I left him a message saying that my uncle was in the hospital and I had to fly home, because they were afraid he wasn't going to make it. This was a lie, but I was trying to buy some time. I thought if I could give myself a few days, somehow I could maybe get at least part of the money back. Of course, I couldn't. That money was long gone. I realized the only way to make $80,000 in a day was to rob a bank, but I decided that was probably not a good idea.

After a few days of hiding out in a shitty motel, I knew I had to tell Kevin what had happened. I was so scared to see him. He had changed my life and done so much for me, so the last thing in the world I wanted to do was upset him. I had become so close with his whole family, and I didn't want to disappoint all of them. They were the big, close family I had always dreamed of having, and I felt so lucky that they let me be a small part of it. Kevin and Oliver both told me countless times, "The only thing you have in the gambling world is your reputation. If your reputation is gone, you are gone." I drove around and around his neighborhood like a scared NASCAR driver. I just couldn't make myself park in front of his house. I eventually parked down the street from it and just sat in the car (the car he had given me). I cried for almost an hour. I would open my car door and then shut it. Open it, shut it, open it, shut it, open it, shut it. Every time I thought I finally had myself together and was ready to go face the music, I would open the door, and before I could start to get out, I was crying again. I physically couldn't get out of the car.

Finally, I got the courage to get out, and I walked slowly down the street to his house. I walked in the back door hoping that nobody would be home and I could just get back in my car and leave. Of course, I wasn't that lucky. When I opened the door, Kevin and his three sons were lying around the living room watching football. The kids all yelled, "BRANDT!" and were so excited to see me. I hadn't been to the house in almost a week, and they were used to seeing me daily. The second Kevin and I made eye contact he knew something was wrong. My eyes were red and puffy from sitting outside crying, and I am sure he could see the fear in my face. He immediately stood up and asked if I was okay, and I said, "Yeah, but can I talk to you real quick?" We walked back into his office. As soon as he shut the door, I started crying uncontrollably. With tears streaming down my face, I told him everything that happened. I told him that I swear I didn't mean for it to happen, and I know I should have watched the money better. That I tried so hard to get the money back, and we even tried to kill my dad.

I was so worried that he was going to be mad at me, but he wasn't. In true Kevin fashion, he came over and put his hand on my shoulder and said, "Stop crying, it's okay. I know you didn't do it and I understand. Desperate people do desperate things." He said, "In the future please don't try to kill anybody, because that will cause a ton of problems for all of us. If you have any problems, always come to me and I will take care of them. I am sorry your dad did this to you and your brother. He has a problem and needs help. Don't worry, we can always make more money. I will explain everything to Oliver and we will get you back to work tomorrow." I was also scared Oliver was going to be mad at me, but the next day when I walked into the office, he gave me a big hug and said, "Sorry about your shitty dad. Fuck him. We are always here for your kid—now let's get you back to work!" He handed me $100,000 cash and asked, "you don't have any other dads we need to worry about do you?" It was the perfect joke, because there was so much tension in the room. That joke made everybody laugh and relax. I went back to work that afternoon, and not a word was ever said about my dad again.

Kevin and Oliver were both great business men, but I would say their best quality was that they were both amazing dads. They would do anything for their kids. From that day on, Kevin treated me like his fourth son. I would spend all of the holidays with his family, buy him Father's Day gifts, and go on family vacations with them. He was a lot like Ron, and they both were the dad I always wanted. After my dad robbed us, one of the first things Kevin said was, "We can always make more money," and boy, was he was right! Over the next couple years, we made a ton of money, and we made it fast. Kevin and Oliver started working with the best hockey handicapper in the world, and he was a gold mine. At the time, the casinos weren't really that interested in hockey, because nobody really bet on it. A few drunk, Canadian tourists would bet 50-100 bucks each day, but that was about the only action they would get. Hockey season takes place at the same time as Pro Football, College Football, Pro Basketball, and College Basketball, which are the four main sports everybody bets. The sports book was worried about those games, so we were killing them on hockey, and nobody even noticed. They would only let us bet two to five thousand a game, depending on the casino, but when you are winning a majority of the games you bet, the winnings add up fast.

Over time, I became part of the company, instead of just an employee on salary. Kevin and Oliver gave me 3% of whatever we won each week in hockey, so that made me work even harder on the streets. They also gave me a lot more responsibilities in the daily operations of the company. One of my new jobs was doing what they called P&C's every Tuesday afternoon. P&C stands for pay and collect, so if we owed somebody money, I would meet them in a parking lot and hand them a brown paper bag full of money. If they owed us, they would meet me and give me a brown paper bag full of money. I would park in the back of a grocery store parking lot and wait for random cars to pull up next to me. We would both roll down our driver's side windows, and a very quick transaction was made, usually with very little conversation. Sometimes I knew the guys, and sometimes I didn't. It was always a little nerve-racking, but luckily I never had any problems.

One of the coolest perks of doing P&Cs was that sometimes the people that owed us money didn't live in Las Vegas. If they lived in another state, I would fly to wherever they were and pick up the cash in a grocery store parking lot in their town. It was usually just a one day trip, with me leaving bright and early in the morning, meeting with them around noon, and then flying back to Vegas in time to meet my bosses at dinner and give them the package full of money. I loved these trips, because they would pay for all expenses and give me an extra $500 just for going. My favorite trips were to Colorado, because they would let me spend the night and turn it into a mini, one-day romantic vacation. I would fly to Denver to meet an ex-Denver Bronco player, which was really cool, since that was my favorite team growing up. He would always surprise me with some cool Bronco gear hidden in the bag of money. He would give me the package, which was usually somewhere between $50,000 and $100,000 in cash, and then I would go get a suite at a five star hotel and wait for Cameron, who was a beautiful blonde who also grew up in Cheyenne. We dated the summer after graduation, and had recently reconnected. She lived just over two hours north of Denver, so she would drive down and we would have a fancy dinner and spend the night in a beautiful hotel room. In the morning, we would have wild morning hotel sex, breakfast delivered to the room, and then she would head back to college, and I would catch a flight back to Las Vegas.

That was always my favorite day of work... well at least it was before 9/11 happened. About two months after 9/11, I had to fly to Denver to pick up $90,000. I had never experienced any problems with airport security, because back then, it was very relaxed. Before 9/11, I would just put the money in my backpack, my girlfriend would walk me to my gate, give me a big hug and kiss, and I would get on the plane without anybody knowing about the cash jackpot that was attached to my back. But after 9/11, my bosses were nervous about going through security carrying that much cash, so we came up with a plan. I would have Cameron hold the package of money outside the security gate, and I would walk through security without the cash, making sure the metal detectors didn't beep. I would then wait awhile, and then tell security I forgot something important in my car and I had to go back out into the airport concourse. Cameron would be waiting for me in the family restroom, where she would tape the package to my back, and then I would go through security again. We figured it's just money, tape, and a big envelope. None of that should set off the metal detector.

That day, Cameron held the money, and I went through the security checkpoint and it didn't beep. I waited about twenty minutes, and then went back out into the airport to meet Cameron. I went to the restroom where we had planned to meet. I did our secret knock, so she knew it was safe to unlock the door and let me in. The family restroom is the only place where you have any privacy in the airport, so we decided to make that our office for the day. Safe inside, I took off my coat and shirt, and she taped the money tightly to my back. There was a small bump that was visible before I put my coat on, but with the coat on, everything looked normal. Hand in hand, Cameron and I headed back to the gate like Bonnie and Clyde. I wasn't nervous because I thought we had done a good job hiding the package, but Cameron's palm was sweaty. She was really quiet and definitely scared. When we got to the gate, I leaned over and softly whispered into her ear, "Calm down baby, everything will be fine. I got this." I gave her a big hug and a long kiss and walked confidently to the security gate. As I got to the security station, I took one last look over my shoulder and smiled and winked at her, just to let her know everything would be fine. She smiled back and blew me a kiss. I started jumping up and down, pretending like I couldn't catch the kiss, just trying to make her laugh. She did laugh, and I felt like it let her finally relax and stop worrying.

I finally reached the front of the security line again. I was next to go through the metal detector. Just five steps more and I'd be safe. But of course nothing in my life ever goes as I plan. The second I stepped through the metal detector, I heard two loud beeps. When I heard those beeps, my heart started pounding harder than it ever has. I immediately looked over my right shoulder and made eye contact with Cameron, who was about 50 yards away. There was no way she could hear the beeps from where she was standing, but she could see the panic on my face, and it made her start crying. The TSA officer asked me if I have any metal objects on me, and I said, "Nope!" He then asked if I minded if they patted me down, and I said I didn't. He ran his fingers down my arms and legs. Then he slid his hand down my back. When he felt the lump at the small of my back, he stopped. "What is this?" Like an idiot, I replied, "Oh, it's nothing." The TSA officer looked very confused and said, "wait right here for a second," and walked over to his supervisor.

At this point, I should have said something, but I didn't. I guess I thought the supervisor would just look at me as an unthreatening young kid and wave me through. As the supervisor walked over, it looked like the officer was telling him what was going on. "Take off your coat and pull up the back of your shirt," the supervisor said. I took off my coat and sat it on the ground. A crowd of about 25 people had formed, and everybody was watching my every move. I then began to try to explain what was going on, as I slowly pulled up my shirt, but when they saw the taped package, all hell broke loose. The crowd let out a collective loud scream and began to run from the area. The officers pulled out their walkie-talkies and started yelling some weird airport codes and screaming that they had an emergency! Within seconds, I was surrounded by police, and everybody was freaking out. Nobody would get close to me, because they all thought it was a bomb. At this point, I started trying to tell anybody that would listen, "It's not a bomb, It's NOT a bomb, it's just a package for my boss." One brave cop grabbed me by the arm and quickly took me into a security room that was about 30 yards away. When we got into the room, I immediately told the cop that it was just money. I was scared to put it in my bags, because I thought somebody might steal it. I gave them my ID, and they slowly peeled the tape off of my back, removed the package, and left the room. I sat in that room by myself for almost 45 minutes, waiting for the cops to come back. The weird thing is, I didn't even think about getting in trouble with the cops and national security, all I was worried about was that I had fucked up and lost a large amount of money again. Kevin would be furious. That's how much I loved Kevin: in all that chaos and possibly on the verge of serious jail time, all I was thinking was that I just didn't want to disappoint my hero again. Eventually, the cops came back in and gave me back my package. They told me that they had it x-rayed, had opened it and it checked out, and it was simply cash, just like I said. The cops told me I was a fucking idiot, but I was a fucking idiot that was free to go. I had missed my flight, but I was more than happy to buy a new one. I was relieved that I wasn't going to jail, and more importantly, I hadn't lost Kevin's money again. In hindsight, I realized I overthought the whole thing. If there is one city in America you can fly to with a whole bunch of cash, it's Las Vegas.

I only picked up money a couple more times after that incident, but those times I was much better prepared. I ended up buying a big snowboarding vest with a bunch of pockets, and then stashed 10–20 thousand in each pocket. This was a much better plan, because I always had the money attached to me, and I only had to take the vest off for 10 seconds so it could go through the x-ray machine. I am sure this is a problem most people will never have, but if you do, please remember that a vest is my recommendation for the best way to transport large amounts of money through an airport. I did learn a valuable lesson that day, though. Being the guy everybody in the airport thinks has a bomb is the fastest way to become the most hated guy in the airport. I have never had so many adults shake their heads at me in disgust. That day, everybody in the airport thought I was a fucking idiot, and they were all right!

*L*ooking back at that time in my life, I made an inordinate amount of questionable decisions. I blame most of those bad decisions on the money. When you carry that much cash, you develop a confidence that makes you feel like you are invincible. I never hesitated to pull out a huge wad of money, which I quickly learned made people act differently. When you see a 24-year-old kid whip out $20,000 in cash, the power in the room quickly changes. I would always become the alpha male. Most people don't have $20,000 in the bank, and I wasn't hesitating to pull it out of my camouflage cargo shorts at a moment's notice. People were always a lot nicer to me the second they saw the money. I think mostly because they didn't know who I was or why I had it. When people see that much cash, they immediately think you are a celebrity. People would always ask, "Are you famous? Should I know who you are?" I would never tell them the truth. I would just put a big smile on my face, and say, "Oh man, I am nobody too important," and then walk away, letting them wonder about who I really was.

Living in Vegas was the complete opposite of growing up in Cheyenne. I think most people in Wyoming are very

generous, genuine and thoughtful. It seemed like most of the people I met in Vegas were only interested in what others could do for them. I made a lot of acquaintances in Las Vegas, but I only met a few people that I will definitely be friends with for the rest of my life. One of those people is my friend Justin Dupree. We met on the same basketball court I met the gambling crew, but he was just a small town kid from Indiana that came to Las Vegas to go to school at UNLV. He worked as a pizza delivery driver, and we clicked immediately. Anthony and Kevin were both married, and Justin was a young good-looking guy, so he was the perfect beer drinking, sports watching, and lady killing wingman. Casey and Tim were back in Wyoming starting families of their own, so Justin stepped right in and was my new best friend. Justin was one of the very few people I met in Vegas that I loved being around.

On the other end of the spectrum there was a group of people that I hated being around, and unfortunately, I had to see them everyday. That group was the dumbass casino security guards. Nothing upset me more than somebody talking down to me because they were in a shitty suit or had a plastic badge. The security guards would constantly bother me and talk shit because I was in my early 20s, and I guess they thought I was some punk kid on Spring Break. The biggest problem I have with security guards is they act like big shots with all kinds of power, but when you think about it, they actually have no power. It's not a job you work hard for. It's usually a job you take when you can't get anything else. It was very hard to listen to some fat-ass try to boss me around when I had five times what he makes in a year in my pockets. I would fight with these guys every single day, and over time, my frustration hit an all-time high and I just couldn't take it anymore.

I legitimately have around twenty-five legendary stories involving me fighting with these idiots, but I am only going to give you my favorite one in this book. I actually used to tell this story on stage every night, but the casino found out and contacted my agents and management and let them know if I kept telling the story on stage, they were going to sue. So, unfortunately, I can't tell you which casino this story happened at, but I will tell you that the lawyers at the Imperial Palace are fucking assholes.

It was a Friday night in the middle of summer, and my friend John and I were just hanging out at a random, anonymous casino. We actually went there, because we knew this guy named Craig and he had a list of girls and we wanted to meet one! If you have never purchased a girl for 200 roses off Craigslist, then you probably didn't get that little joke. Let me spell it out for you, we were going to get a hooker. I had lived in Las Vegas for almost six years, and I had never purchased a lady of the night. I feel like there are four things you have to do if you visit Las Vegas the second you get into town: 1) you need to take a picture by that dumb sign; 2) you need to see the Bellagio fountains; 3) you need to get drunk and go eat at a shitty buffet; and, 4) you need to get a hooker. I had never had a hooker, and I was always curious what it would be like. There was one big problem; I just love my grandma so much, and I remember when I was 14 years old she pulled me aside and bluntly said, "Brandt don't you ever pay for pussy," which turned out to be great advice. Okay, so maybe it wasn't my Grandma who told me that, but somebody did, and I knew she would be very disappointed in me if she ever found out.

I remember thinking that I didn't want to disappoint my sweet old grandma, so I came up with a plan. I figured if I just won a bunch of money gambling and used that money, it would be like the casino just comped the hooker for me. You know, like a "total rewards hooker!" I don't know why I felt so weird about it, but for some reason, I just felt like I couldn't spend my own money. I decided if I won a couple hundred dollars, I was going to make an hourly purchase. If I lost a couple hundred gambling, I would just go home and sleep alone.

It was around 1 a.m. when I made this important decision, and, needless to say, I was very intoxicated. It was way too late to bet on sports, so I had to hit the tables. The bad news for me (and the hookers) is that I suck at table games. I had played Blackjack over a hundred times, and I swear I lost every single time. But on this night, I felt like there was magic in the air, and that magic was located in a little white ball! My game of choice for the evening was going to be Roulette. I sat down at the far end of the table, bought $100 worth of light blue chips, and started ordering double Red Bull and vodkas for me and John. It turned out it actually was my lucky night because the second I sat down, I got on a hot streak. I hit the first two numbers I played and was up $400 in the first five minutes. Over the next 35 minutes, my money went up and down as the game got going fast. At one point, I looked down and saw stacks and stacks of chips and decided I should stop for a minute and see how much I had won. I counted up my chips and realized that I had turned my $100 buy-in into almost $1800. I turned to John and said, "HOLY SHIT! This is the best night of my life!"

Seconds after I said that, the pit boss came over, tapped me on the shoulder, and said, "Hey! Hey! You can't be talking like that." I was stunned. I turned around and said, "What are you talking about?"

"You can't be saying shit in my casino."

Confused, I replied, "It's like 2 a.m. There are hookers, people doing blow, and everybody in here is drunk, and you are telling me I can't say shit?"

"I told you once, boy, I am not going to tell you again, you say shit one more time and you are out of here."

"Okay," I said, "That's fair. But since you just said it too, if you say shit one more time, then YOU are out of here!" Everybody at the table thought this was hilarious. The pit boss didn't agree. He immediately called the security guards, and the next thing I knew, here came five security guards waddling over. It's hard for them to walk when they are carrying all of their broken dreams. I assume these security guards wanted to be real police officers, but they couldn't, because they had a 3rd-grade education and ran a 27-minute mile. I suddenly found myself dealing with five security guards, because I had said "shit" in a casino at 2 a.m. The lead security guard approached me with his fat chest puffed out, and said, "Hey kid, is there some kind of problem here?"

"YES!" I replied. "You dumbasses are bothering me for no reason!"

At that moment, his partner stepped up and, in his best tough guy voice, yelled, "You want us to call our sergeant! You want the Sarg to come over here and kick your little ass outta here?"

"Yeah," I said. "Call the Sergeant." I then asked John, "I wonder how you become the sergeant of casino security? I bet you just have to get a shitty suit, some batting gloves, and then tell 200 people where the bingo room is located!"

We both laughed out loud as I chugged my half glass of red bull vodka and sat the empty glass down on the table. When I looked up, guess who I saw...yep, the fat ass Sarg waddling over with five more security guards. At  this point, we have ten security guards and a Sergeant, all because I said shit in a casino at 2 a.m. The security guards took my Wyoming ID and walked it over to the sergeant. The sergeant pulled out his reading glasses from the inside pocket of his shitty plaid sport coat and thoroughly inspected my ID. He examined both the front and back, bent it back and fourth, and then picked at the corners to make sure it was real.

He then walked over to me, handed me back my Wyoming ID, and asked me, "Hey boy, where you from?" I was very confused, since he had just been looking at my Wyoming ID for the last five minutes. I shook my head, very annoyed, and replied, "I am from Wyoming." He replied, "Well, I don't know how you talk to your little sheep girlfriend back in Wyoming, but you are not going to say shit in front of women in my casino." Now, that's obviously an awful joke, but all the dumbass security guards thought it was so funny. They laughed. Their laughter gave the sergeant confidence, and he just stood there three feet

in front of me, staring at me with the biggest smile on his face. I didn't laugh at all. I didn't have any jokes in the moment, so I just decided to hit them with some brutal honesty. I said, "Sir, I don't ever like to curse in front of women, but I do know a group of women who curse every single morning. It's your mothers, when they wake up and think, "my son is a 47-year-old security guard in Las Vegas... SHIT!" John and I thought this was hilarious, but the security guards didn't think I was nearly as funny as their Sarg! The sergeant said, "That's it smartass, take your chips to the cage, cash them out, and then get the hell out of my casino! I said, "Okay, you got it buddy," but then I looked around and saw a huge crowd had formed because there were so many security guards surrounding me.

These fat ass security guards had pissed me off and ruined my hooker dreams. At this point I was way too mad too have sex; all I wanted was revenge. On my way to the casino cage, I passed the roulette table and the pit boss that started all of this. The pit boss was standing there with an arrogant look on his face, suggesting he had beaten me, but what he didn't know was this game was not quite over yet. I walked right up to his roulette table (and if you know anything about roulette, you know there is the wheel and then in front of the wheel, there is over $100,000 in casino chips). I got to the table and reached in for a stack of chips, but then I thought at the last second, "Fuck it, I don't want this money," and I reached right over the chips and stopped the spinning wheel with my left hand. As the roulette ball continued to bounce around, I snatched it up with my right hand and took it off of the table. I was now standing there holding the little white ball, and everybody in the casino pretty much stopped in their tracks waiting to see what I would do next.

All the drunk tourists were looking at me like I was holding a miniature time bomb. Just like when I was a kid, I decided if I can't play, then I am taking my ball, and I am going home. But as I held the ball, I realized I didn't even want that stupid white marble. I looked at the pit boss, and he was just looking at me with a look of shock on his face. At this point, there was only one thing to do. I took all my drunk anger, reared back, and threw that ball as hard as I could at the pit boss. BOOM! Right in the chest!

This is when the whole night gets a little blurry. The next thing I knew, those fat ass security guards tackled me in the middle of the casino. I landed hard on the right side of my face, and then we wrestled around for about 45 seconds. When I hit the floor, I chipped a tooth, and my watch broke into what felt like twenty pieces. They had me pinned face-down on the dirty ass casino carpet, and they zip-tied my hands up behind my back. I laid there for about ten minutes, with some fat boy's knee in my back. The sergeant stood over me, talking shit to me the whole time.

When they finally let me stand up, the crowd went crazy! The few older people that were still awake were yelling things like "get him out of here, he is a nuisance," and the drunk, young people were screaming things like "OH MY GOD, that shit was crazy, you are a legend!" I had about 15 security guards escorting me through the casino and up the elevators to casino jail. Casino jail actually wasn't that bad. It was a much nicer room than any of the shitty hotel rooms they gave their guests. They told me I had to stay in their little, fake jail until the real cops came to get me.

For the next two hours, as we waited for the cops to arrive, I spent every minute talking shit to any security guard that was brave enough to come in the room. I had so much fun asking them questions like, "Why do you need Nike wristbands to match your uniform? When did you give up on your dreams? What time does your mommy drop you off for work in the morning?" Eventually, two Las Vegas Metro Police Officers showed up, and I don't mess with real cops. I have a ton of respect for those guys, plus these two cops were huge. The security guards told the cops the whole story, and the cops said, "Okay we will take it from here." They asked me to stand up, clipped off the zip ties, and put me in real handcuffs. I was now terrified. I had never been to jail in my life. My first thought was, "what if I get in there and I see my dad?!"

The cops said, "Alright kid, let's go" and we walked down this long hallway, which felt like it was 50 miles long. The cops didn't say one word to each other or me the whole walk. I will never forget how quiet and dark that hallway was. I could hear every step I took, and I knew each step was getting me closer to jail. We eventually got to a huge cargo elevator, and I got in and stood right in the middle. The cops got in, and one stood on each side of me like I was a killer. You would have thought that I played tight end for the New England Patriots, or something. We rode the elevator down five floors in total silence, and then the door opened to the loud casino floor. We all got out of the elevator, and one of the cops told me to sit down at the slot machine right by the front doors. The two cops then walked about 30 feet away and talked for a couple minutes. I was scared, because the last thing I wanted to do was go to jail in downtown Vegas. It was now around 4 in the morning, and I wasn't sure who I could call at that time of night to come bail me out.

The bigger of the two cops started to walk over, and I could feel my legs shaking. I was sitting down at a slot machine looking up at him, and he was standing over me. He was about 6'7 and was one of the most intimidating men I have ever seen. He looked down at me with no emotion on his face and said, "Hey man, I have been doing this job 17 years...and that is the greatest fucking story I have ever heard." The biggest smile came over his face. He then took off my handcuffs and said, "We are going to give you a ticket, but you don't have to worry about it, because we won't show up for court, and the casino definitely can't pay all of those people involved to take a day off work and go to court. So you are now free to go, just don't ever come back to this casino again." I was shocked, and realized that even though I didn't get to have sex with a hooker, it was still a very lucky night. I said, "Thank you so much, sir, I promise I will never come back here again." I then walked out the front doors as fast as I could.

In my office, I have awards, pictures with celebrities, my D.A.R.E. certificate, and my fake college degree all hanging proudly on my wall, but nobody gives a shit about any of that. The only thing anybody ever wants to talk about is the pink ticket I have framed above my desk from the Las Vegas Metropolitan Police Department that reads: "Disturbing the peace- Stopping live roulette game in progress and hitting pit boss in the chest with a roulette ball." It has done way more for my career than some stupid college degree. My advice (if you have kids and you think they are going to struggle in college and waste all of your hard earned money), just give them a couple hundred dollars, send them to Vegas, and tell them to make an unbelievable story!

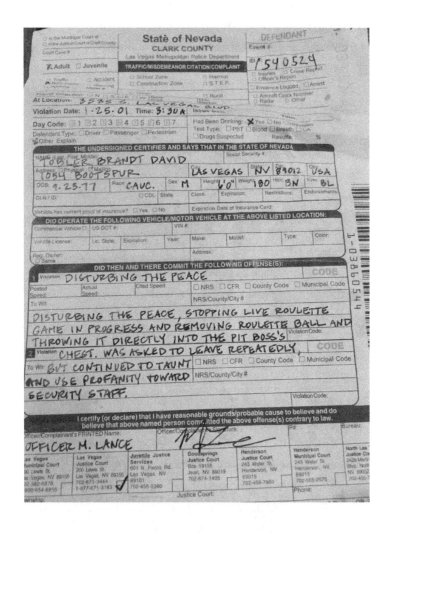

State of Nevada
CLARK COUNTY
Las Vegas Metropolitan Police Department
TRAFFIC/MISDEMEANOR CITATION/COMPLAINT

☐ In the Municipal Court of
☐ In the Justice Court of Clark County
Court Case #

☒ Adult ☐ Juvenile

DEFENDANT
Event #
ID: 1540524

☐ School Zone ☐ Hazmat
☐ Construction Zone ☐ S.T.E.P.

☐ Traffic ☐ Accident

☐ Injuries ☐ Crime Report
☐ Officer's Report
☐ Evidence Logged ☐ Arrest
☐ Aircraft Clock Number
☐ Radar ☐ Other

At Location: 3535 S LAS VEGAS BLVD

Violation Date: 1-25-01 Time: 3:30 A Issue

Day Code: ☐1 ☐2 ☐3 ☐4 ☐5 ☐6 ☐7
Defendant Type: ☐Driver ☐Passenger ☐Pedestrian
☒Other Explain.

Had Been Drinking: ☒Yes ☐No
Test Type: ☐PBT ☐Blood ☐Breath ☐UA
☐Drugs Suspected   Results   %

THE UNDERSIGNED CERTIFIES AND SAYS THAT IN THE STATE OF NEVADA

NAME (Last, First, Middle): TOBLER BRANDT DAVID   Social Security #:

Address: ☐Physical ☐Mailing 1054 BOOTSPUR   City: LAS VEGAS   State: NV   Zip: 89012   Cty: USA

DOB: 9-25-77   Race: CAUC.   Sex: M   Height: 6'0"   Weight: 180   Hair: BN   Eyes: BL

OLN / ID: ☐CDL State: Class: Expiration: Restrictions: Endorsements:

Vehicle has current proof of insurance? ☐Yes ☐No   Expiration Date of Insurance Card:

DID OPERATE THE FOLLOWING VEHICLE/MOTOR VEHICLE AT THE ABOVE LISTED LOCATION:

Commercial Vehicle ☐ US DOT #:   VIN #:

Vehicle License: Lic. State: Expiration: Year: Make: Model: Type: Color:

Reg. Owner:
☐Same   Address:

DID THEN AND THERE COMMIT THE FOLLOWING OFFENSE(S):

1 Violation: DISTURBING THE PEACE   CODE

Posted Speed: Actual Speed: Cited Speed: ☐NRS ☐CFR ☐County Code ☐Municipal Code

To Wit: NRS/County/City #

DISTURBING THE PEACE, STOPPING LIVE ROULETTE
GAME IN PROGRESS AND REMOVING ROULETTE BALL AND
THROWING IT DIRECTLY INTO THE PIT BOSS'S   Violation Code:

2 Violation: CHEST. WAS ASKED TO LEAVE REPEATEDLY,   CODE

To Wit: BUT CONTINUED TO TAUNT   NRS/County/City #
AND USE PROFANITY TOWARD
SECURITY STAFF.   Violation Code:

I certify (or declare) that I have reasonable grounds/probable cause to believe and do
believe that above named person committed the above offense(s) contrary to law.

Officer/Complainant's PRINTED Name: OFFICER M. LANCE   Officer/Complainant's Signature: P#:   Bureau:

| Las Vegas Municipal Court 00 Lewis St. Las Vegas, NV 89105 702-382-6878 800-654-6856 | Las Vegas Justice Court 200 Lewis St. Las Vegas, NV 89155 702-671-3444 1-877-671-3183 | Juvenile Justice Services 601 N. Pecos Rd. Las Vegas, NV 89101 702-455-5360 | Goodsprings Justice Court Box 19155 Jean, NV 89019 702-874-1405 | Henderson Justice Court 243 Water St. Henderson, NV 89015 702-455-7980 | Henderson Municipal Court 243 Water St. Henderson, NV 89015 702-455-2076 | North Las Vegas Justice Court 2428 Martin Blvd. North NV 89032 702-455-7 |

Justice Court: Phone:

You are probably wondering if I ever went back to the Imperial Palace. Of course I did! I was back in there two days later. Casinos do have a lot of rules, but the one thing they like more than rules is money. After this incident, I had a meeting with the casino higher ups, and they promised me the security guards would never bother me again. They also made me promise to try not to be a drunk asshole in their casino. We both agreed that was a fair deal, and I never caused, nor had another problem at the fabulous Imperial Palace.

They only made this deal because I was very valuable to the casino sports book. Even though we were one of the few people beating them out of money, they needed our information. We let them know where their odds should be at all times. For example, I had a limit on everything I bet. The most I could bet on an NFL game was $20,000. If I bet $20,000, they would immediately take down the game and adjust the line. When I made a bet, they knew somebody might be hurt, or the weather might be changing, or it could be one of countless other important things. They didn't always know exactly what it meant, but they knew that game needed their attention immediately. The casino would take their time putting the line back up for other people to bet, until they figured out why we bet what we did. A lot of times I would bet $20,000 on a game, and once they gave me my ticket, I would say, "Hey be careful on that game. We don't think a certain player is going to play."

Yeah, it sucks that we got an obvious advantage on our $20,000 dollar bet, but that protected them from another wise guy putting one of his friends in a fancy suit, getting him drunk, and having him stumble up there, pretending like a rich tourist wasted on vacation trying to bet $200,000 like a sucker. There was a lot of gamesmanship in the gambling world, but in the end, we scratched their backs, and they scratched ours. There was enough room for us to make a pretty good chunk of change from the casino, and that, in turn, helped the casino make billions of dollars from the public. Building these relationships with the sports book supervisors allowed me to make a ton of money for Kevin and Oliver, and some nights it allowed me to make a bunch of money for myself.

Without going into too much detail to keep everybody out of trouble, there were a couple nights when I just couldn't lose. Wink! Wink! You would be surprised how much money you can win when you are able to bet a game when 85% of that game is over. A couple of the sportsbook employees occasionally let me do some very illegal shit, because they just hated the way their bosses treated them. I was really good at picking the winner when one team was up by 17 with two minutes left to play. It goes back to the message I repeat again and again in this book. If you own a business, you better treat your employees well, because if you don't, when you are spending all day trying to beat your competition, they will spend all day trying to beat you.

The next few years in Vegas are one big blur. I could write ten books with the stories I have from the wild nights full of expensive dinners, Russian cocktail waitresses, hookers, massage parlors, wild hotel sex with tourists, and all the booze my friends and I could drink! The best thing about it was that I was betting so much money, I could get pretty much all of my food, booze, and hotels comped. These casinos became huge adult playgrounds for my friends and me, and there was no better feeling than having the ability to do whatever I wanted, whenever I wanted. I was having so much fun that I would sometimes spend a week at a casino instead of making the fifteen-minute drive to my house. When we were really winning I would party all night, pass out in a big suite, wake up, and stumble across the street to the mall to buy brand new clothes for the day.

I was living my life like a rich, drunk, twelve year old! I had transformed from a goofy, broke, kid in Wyoming, into a fearless, rich, maniac in a city with no rules. How fearless you ask? Well, I broke into Mike Tyson's house long before they ever did it in the hilarious movie The Hangover. Let me explain… When I moved to Las Vegas, I lived right by Mike Tyson's gated 12,000 sq. foot mansion, and I would drive by every day hoping to see him. He was my all-time favorite boxer growing up, and when you live in Wyoming, you never get to see celebrities. (Luke Perry did come to my town one year, and twenty-five years later people are still talking about it). In hindsight, I don't really know why I thought Iron Mike would just be hanging out in his driveway selling lemonade or mowing his lawn, but regardless, I drove by his house every single day. I actually couldn't even see his front yard, because he had huge 15-foot walls around his property. He also had a security guard (a huge black guy who always wore camouflage cargo pants and a black shirt) standing outside his front gate. Every day I would drive by, and every day he looked like he wanted to murder me. But one day, I drove by and he was gone. He wasn't there the next day either. I drove by every day that week looking for him, and he was never there. The following week I drove by the house, and there was a For Sale sign in front of the gate and still no guard! I told myself this was my chance. I figured I would just climb over the gate, and if anybody stopped me, I would show them I had a ton of cash on me and tell them I was seriously considering buying the mansion. I know, I know, another dumbass plan.

So, I jumped over the gate and started to slowly walk around the property like a very scared, but interested, possible buyer. As I explored, I saw so many amazing things that really made me want to buy the house. There were tiger cages, a basketball court, an incredible pool with a slide and secret grotto, countless garages, and an enormous religious statue. I went to the back of the house and messed with the door a little bit, and boom, the next thing I knew I was in Mike Tyson's house! I tiptoed in and sheepishly yelled, "Hello? Is anybody here?" I was scared to death that Mike would jump out at any second and break my face. I took about five soft steps into a very empty family room, and

INSURANCE IDENTIFICATION CARD

State	NV	
Company	Progressive	
Policy Number	Effective Date	Expiration Date
CA 04340958-0	8/17/00	8/17/01
Year Make/Model		Vehicle Identification Number
1989 Mercedes Benz 560 SEL C		WDBCA39E4KA440177
Agency/Company Issuing Card		
	W.M. Roche & Associates	
	1-800-325-2077	
Insured	Mike Tyson Enterprises, Inc.	
	6740 Tomiyasu Lane	
	Las Vegas, NV 89120	

all of a sudden, I heard a loud beep. I froze dead in my tracks. Then I took another couple steps, and I heard the loud beep again. That second beep freaked me out, and I ran out the back door, jumped the wall, and got the hell out of there. I drove straight to Justin's house and told him the whole story. He told me I was out of my mind, and if the champ found me in his house he would destroy me! That night, I was lying in bed thinking about the whole day, and all of a sudden, I heard that same beeping sound that I had heard earlier in the day in Tyson's house. I thought, "Oh my god somebody from Mike Tyson's house is in my house, and they are going to kill me!!!" I laid there for a couple minutes with my head under the covers like a six-year-old scared of the boogie monster, but I kept hearing the beeping. At one point, I realized I had nothing to worry about. The beeps were coming from the smoke detector in the hallway that must have been out of batteries. This made perfect sense. Mike Tyson had moved out weeks prior, so there was nobody in his house to change the batteries in his smoke detectors. That meant I had nothing to worry about when I was in his house.

The next day, I woke up very excited, and I immediately drove to Justin's house to tell him the whole story about the smoke detectors and convince him to come with me to Tyson's house. He was a little hesitant at first, but after 10 minutes of me promising Justin that I would take Tyson's first punch if we ran into him, he was in. We wanted to document our journey, so we drove to Target, bought two disposable cameras, and we were on our way to the champ's compound. We parked a half mile away, waited for there to be no traffic, hopped the front gate then headed straight for the back door. Just like the day before, I was able to mess with the lock and get us in the back door, and without a hitch, we were inside Mike Tyson's house! We were both very scared, but as we walked around the house, it became very obvious that he had moved out. There was nothing left except big items, like couches, a gigantic entertainment center, and a beautiful black grand piano. (I later found out the piano was a gift from Stevie Wonder.) There were a few boxes of little things spread throughout the house that seemed like stuff that needed to be thrown away.

For the next three hours, we opened every closet, kitchen drawer, and cabinet in the house, trying to find a jackpot. When you break into Mike Tyson's house, you have to steal something to prove you were there. We wanted a championship belt, a big bag of cash, or part of somebody's ear! But unfortunately, we didn't find much. The coolest thing we found was the title to a custom built, white, four-door convertible Mercedes that was parked in the garage.

Ironically, he left a George Foreman grill in the kitchen, and we had to take that, because we thought it was hilarious to have Tyson's-Foreman grill. We didn't find anything of real value, and we were close to giving up, but then we thought we hit a miracle.

We were snooping around in his TV room, and he had this huge couch with a matching ottoman. I recognized the pattern on the couch and ottoman, and I told Justin, "We should steal that ottoman. It's Versace, and it's probably worth a couple thousand bucks."

"How do you know its Versace?" He said.

"That weird face symbol is the logo for Versace." He asked me if I was sure and I said, "Watch this." I picked up the ottoman to look on the bottom of it for a Versace tag, and as I picked the ottoman up, a VHS tape fell out of the inside of the ottoman and bounced twice on the floor. Justin and I just looked at each other like, "HOLY SHIT, we just found a hidden videotape in Mike Tyson's house!" We figured it had to be a tape of him doing something awful, like killing somebody, or even better, a sex tape! Our first thought was that we would sell this tape for millions and get rich. We took that VHS tape, jumped the wall in a single bounce, ran down the block, and hopped into my car. I drove home as fast as I could, and we spent the whole ride home discussing whether we were going to buy a yacht, a helicopter, or maybe even a yacht we could land a helicopter on!

Unfortunately, when we got home and watched our secret million dollar tape, we were very disappointed to find out it was just a video of Mike making a video game, and talking about how he hates white people (which was not exactly breaking news). We spent the rest of that summer partying in Mike Tyson's backyard pool and grotto. It was a hard sales pitch to get girls to believe it was safe, but when we finally got them and the cooler full of alcohol over the wall, we had our own little millionaire backyard playground. We would swim naked, play basketball naked, and just try not to make too much naked-noise! Wayne Newton lived next door, and we had a feeling he would ruin our party if he knew we were his new neighbors. Voluntarily house-sitting Mike Tyson's five million dollar mansion was one of the best summers of my life. I have always loved Mike Tyson, and, ironically, my life was about to go down the same path as Iron Mike's did. I was about to get into a huge fight with my boss, date all the wrong girls, and lose all of my money over and over again. Okay, okay. Maybe the Mike Tyson comparison is a bit of a stretch, but just like the champ, I felt like I was invincible and on top of the world. I had no idea that my personal Buster Douglas was on his way to knock me out and start my downward spiral.

I came into work very hungover one Monday afternoon and was shocked when I was told that we hired somebody new, and it was going to be my job to train her starting early next week. What really confused me was when he said "her." Everybody that worked for us was a dude, and I had no idea why they would want a girl out on the streets carrying that much money. I remember asking Kevin, "This is a joke right?" He said, "Nope, it's real, but she is just going to work with us a couple days a week for the next two months." He continued, "You know who she is. It's "Hot Shannon." Shannon was a family friend of Kevin's that was home for the summer from college. I had actually never met her, but I had heard all about the legendary "HOT Shannon" for the last three years. Kevin and his sons all swore she was the most beautiful girl in Vegas and would be the perfect girl to marry. She knew Kevin loved her, so it only took her one phone call and she was hired. We definitely didn't need her, and she would be awful at the job, but there are some girls in this world that men just can't say no to, and Shannon was definitely one of them.

I was told that Shannon would come with me every day for the first couple of weeks until she got the hang of things. All the guys in the office told me how lucky I was to get to spend every day with her. They even suggested I work for free those weeks, because they would pay money just to be around her. Those same idiots were also quick to remind me that I had absolutely no shot with her! All I knew about her was that she was beautiful, classy, a high school valedictorian, and worst of all, Mormon. I agreed that I probably had no shot with her, and told them I wouldn't be interested in her even if she wanted me. At that time, I was newly single, and into dating strippers, while also trying to have random sex every night with as many different young, drunk tourists that I could meet. My daily goal was to be a part of some sorority girl's crazy Vegas story! A brilliant, extremely religious, very responsible virgin was the exact opposite of what I was looking for.

But the male ego is strong, and the more they told me I couldn't do it, the more it made me want to try. I always liked being the underdog in life, and my confidence was at an all-time high, so I decided I was going to go for it. Then I saw her. The second I saw her, I knew I had no chance. She was breathtakingly beautiful. She had this incredible, long, blonde hair, a perfect smile, an amazing body, and was also so sweet. I was super awkward the first couple days, because I was so nervous. I was second-guessing every dumb thing that came out of my stupid mouth. Eventually, I calmed down and was able to form a full sentence, and even began to make her laugh a little bit. I trained her for three weeks, and every night when we got off work, I would return home and anxiously count down the hours until I could see her again.

We slowly became friends, and it was awesome. Everyday, Kevin and Oliver would ask if I was making any progress with her, and I would say, "Guys, she is so cool. She is honestly like a sister to me. I would never try to hook up with her," which is the same thing every dumb high school kid says about the girl he really likes but knows he can never date. After three weeks of training, Shannon was on her own, and work was now shitty for me, because I didn't get to see her every day. After her first week of work, she called me to give me an update. She was so excited because she got her first paycheck (and of course she got a bonus for hard work... aka being hot) and she asked me if she could take me out to dinner as a thank you for training her. Of course I said yes. The second we hung up the phone, I drove straight to the mall to get a new outfit. I wanted to look good for our first date! I knew it wasn't technically a date, but I was allowed to pretend it was.

That night, she picked me up and we headed to the Sunset Station Casino. I don't know how much her bonus was, but I was shocked she was taking me to one of the nicest steakhouses in town. We both enjoyed big juicy steaks and finished the meal with Bananas Foster, my favorite dessert. We ended up staying at our table and talking for almost two hours after she paid our bill (I tried to pick up the tab, but she told me she would make me walk home if I did). The manager eventually came over and asked us to wrap it up, because they wanted to close and go home. We were both shocked; we were having so much fun that we lost all track of time. She drove me back to my house, and when we got to my driveway, I gave her a hug and was in the process of saying some long, awkward, awful thank you for dinner, when out of nowhere, she asked if she could come in and see the house. This was the house that we used as our office, and she said she just wanted to see where all the phone calls and orders came from each day.

So, we walked up the driveway and into the house. I gave her the full tour, showing her everything except my bedroom, because I was embarrassed that it was such a mess. The tour concluded in the main office, where we sat at our boss's desk and pretended we were in charge for almost an hour. I acted like I was Oliver and she played Kevin. Even though our impressions were awful, they were making us laugh. Once again, we had lost all track of time, and all of a sudden, Shannon realized it was a little past 3 am. She said, "Oh crap, it's late, I better get home." I agreed and said, "let me walk you out." When we got to the front door, I gave her a big hug, and thanked her again for such a fun night. Then we stood there in silence. To my amazement, she said, "Are you going to kiss me or not?" I couldn't believe it! I said, "YES!" which came out a lot louder then I wished it would have. I was way too excited! I leaned in and gave her a soft, long kiss. Then she grabbed my hand, and we walked to her car. She got in, and before she shut her car door, she said, "I had so much fun tonight, can we please do it again tomorrow?" "YES!" I replied, again way too loud.

I stood in the driveway with a huge smile on my face, waving at her as she headed home. As soon as she turned the corner on my street and I could no longer see her car, I sprinted back inside my house, dove on the couch, and let out the loudest happiest scream of my life. I then went and called Kevin. He didn't answer, because it was close to 4 a.m., but I left him the longest, loudest message that started with me screaming, "David kissed Goliath, David kissed Goliath! You guys said it was impossible, but I did it!" I know it was an awful analogy, but he knew what I meant. I didn't fall asleep that morning until around 6, because I was so happy.

The next day when I got to the office, I couldn't wait to brag about kissing Shannon and tell them all about our date. I anticipated a lot of jealousy and shit talking, but everybody was genuinely happy for me. I think they could tell I was glowing. That night, we had a second date and it went great, so we ended up hanging out every night for the next two weeks. After a midnight walk through her neighborhood, we ended up sitting on her back porch, where we finally decided to make it official and tell the world that we were boyfriend and girlfriend. Dating Shannon changed my whole life. I traded in the wild Vegas nights for Mormon

family nights. I needed a break from the strip, and I enjoyed being a part of their loving family atmosphere. Shannon had amazing parents, three awesome brothers, and the cutest little sister. The whole family welcomed me with open arms and I loved spending every free moment at their house. The beers, tequila shots, and hookers were replaced with amazing desserts, movie nights, and a lot of dry humping.

For the next year, I spent every day I could with Shannon, and my life really went through some major changes. I spent less and less time with Kevin and his family, because their lives were also changing. The boys were now all teenagers and were busy doing their own things. Kevin was in the process of finalizing a divorce, and he also began dating somebody new. Kevin had met a new girl who was beautiful, funny, and 15 years younger than him. We were both head over heels in love, and we each thought we had found the girls we would spend the rest of our lives with. The only bad part was that we started seeing other less and less. We would still meet at the gym three times a week, and text throughout the day, but we didn't hang out that much at night, because we were both busy doing whatever our girlfriends had planned for us.

I was in love with Shannon and knew that someday I wanted to marry her, but I wasn't Mormon. Shannon had two goals in life: get married in the temple and become a mother. There was no doubt in my mind that she would be an amazing wife and mother, and I knew I could never do better. So I decided I would meet with the missionaries and begin the process of becoming Mormon. It was an easy decision for me, because I was in madly in love with her and wanted to give her everything she wanted. I wasn't raised with any religion in my life growing up, so part of me was actually excited and fascinated to learn something new. There was a very large Mormon population in Cheyenne when I was growing up, and I spent a lot of time hanging out at my Mormon friends' houses. Every Mormon family I knew was very close, and all I really wanted was a real family. I loved how Shannon's family treated each other, and I wanted them to replace my dad's side of the family since I didn't talk to any of them.

Her family invited me to come to church with them, and after the service, Shannon and I sat down with the bishop and he answered some of the questions I had about the Mormon religion. At the end of our meeting I told him I was very interested in joining the church, and that I would love to start the process. The bishop said he would send the missionaries over the next day, and I could start doing the discussions. Missionary discussions are six lessons that you go through to become a member of the LDS church. I did the first three discussions and I learned a little bit. The missionaries kept telling me that I would start to feel something, but honestly I didn't feel anything. The only thing I remember feeling was that they sure talk about tithing (giving 10% of your income to the church) a lot.

The first big problem I had with the Mormon Church is that they sent two 18-year-olds from South Dakota to tell me, at 28-years old, what I needed to do with the rest of my life. What do these two 18-year-olds know about anything? Every time I would finish a discussion, Shannon would ask what I thought, and I would lie and say I was learning a lot and enjoyed meeting with the missionaries. When they came over to my house for the fourth lesson, the missionaries came in, sat down on the couch, and one of them begin passionately telling me exactly what I needed to do to have an amazing LDS life. Unfortunately, I couldn't take him seriously, because in my head I was laughing my ass off. The kid had been in my house for almost 15 minutes, and he had forgotten to take his bike helmet off. Now, I will admit, I don't know much, but what I do know is you never take life advice from a man wearing a helmet indoors.

Shannon was such an amazing girl, but after that fourth discussion, I told her I just couldn't do the Mormon thing. She said she appreciated me trying and was really sorry I didn't have better missionaries. She still dreamed of getting married in the temple and didn't know what other options she had, so she set up a meeting with her bishop. Her dumbass bishop told her that if she got married, it had to be in the temple. Since I stopped taking the discussions, I could not join her in the temple, so she needed to break up with me. The bishop went so far as to tell her she had to break up with me, because that is what the Lord wanted her to do. It was definitely not what the Brandt wanted her to do. Unfortunately, she listened to this awful advice and broke up with me the next week. I was crushed and fell into a deep depression. There is never a good time to have your heart broken, but this was definitely the wrong time. As Shannon was breaking up with me, the poker boom was just hitting on TV. Kevin was an amazing poker player, and that is how he originally made a ton of his money. He began playing poker full time, which made it hard for him to have time to also bet on sports. He said he preferred to play poker, because he felt like he could somewhat control the outcomes of those games. At the time, every male in the world between 18 and 65 had caught the poker bug, and they were all in a hurry to go to the Vegas casinos and give their money away. Kevin was crushing the tourists. He had been playing poker for 35 years, and most of these idiots had been playing maybe 10 months. He felt a lot more confident in his poker skills than trying to figure out what a bunch of dumb college kids were going to do on a windy, cold, Saturday afternoon. I couldn't argue with that.

The poker boom carried over to online gambling, so sports betting was slowly becoming less popular in the casinos. All the action was moving to the sports betting sites online, so there really wasn't much need for me on the streets. With no need to work super hard since they were both rich, Kevin and Oliver decided they would take a six-month break from sports gambling on the streets, and just play poker whenever they wanted. They told me we would start working again when hockey started in the fall. The lease on the work house was in its last month, so I had three weeks to move out and find my own place. I had saved up a little money, but not nearly as much as I should have. I had just assumed I would get paid every week for forever. I had never imagined we would stop betting. We had been betting every day for the last five years. I now had no income and no idea what to do.

When I applied to get my own apartment, I got a nice surprise from the building manager. She informed me that I had one of the worst credit scores she had ever seen. After doing a little research, I found out that even though I had not talked to my dad in years, he decided he was still going to be a part of my life. My own father had taken out multiple credit cards in my name. (Looking back, Brandt Hufendick doesn't sound that bad, compared to Brandt 435-Credit-

Score-Never-get-a-House Tobler). Why couldn't he have just downed that Jamba Juice? I now needed a place to live and knew I had very few options. Once again I was lost, and realized it was time to either make a plan or start taking some serious chances.

IN THE CORNER ALONE

Luckily, Kevin's middle son Nick had just leased an apartment and was looking for a roommate. Nick was seven years younger than me, and I had always treated him like a little brother. I was excited to move in with him, because we always had fun when we were together. Also, he was very good looking and charming, so he always had beautiful girls partying with him. I was fresh off of my break up and completely heartbroken, but I knew exactly what would cheer me up... young, hot, drunk girls. We had a couple great parties the first week I moved in, but then things started to go downhill fast. When I moved in, I had no idea that Nick had started doing some pretty hard drugs over the last couple months. After one month of living with Nick, the fun was over. The hot girls stopped coming over, and he rarely came home. Neither of us was working, and we were both running out of money. We had a spare room that wasn't being used, so we decided to get a roommate. Our first choice was his friend Marcus.

Marcus was a young charming black kid in his early 20s, who instantly brought the fun back into our apartment. The week he moved in, we started having barbecues and theme parties, and our house was packed every night. He bought a 70-inch big screen TV his third day at the apartment, and all of our friends started coming over to watch basketball on the weekends. Nick loved hanging out with Marcus because he always had drugs, but as the days went on, I started to trust Marcus less and less each day. I was really confused, because he didn't have a job, but he always had money. My first thought was that he had to be a drug dealer. Soon, though, I realized that didn't make sense, because I had seen him buying drugs countless times from some of his shady friends. Then when Marcus did have drugs, he would share them with anybody who wanted some. I never saw anybody give him any money for the drugs.

He eventually ran out of money, and I knew that, because stuff started to disappear from my room. It started, when little stuff, like a cup full of change and a cheap watch went missing, but then I started to realize that anytime I left the house for more than an hour, he had been in my room going through my stuff. I would ask him about it, and he would turn into a defensive asshole and tell me I was just blaming him because he was black. He would then tell me it was probably Nick. The problem with that theory, was that most of the time I left the apartment, Nick was with me. I was really starting to hate Marcus. He was a lying, stealing, drug addicted asshole who reminded me of my dad. I would watch him charm people everyday. Then the second they let their guard down he robbed them. Even after calling him out, he was still constantly trying to rob me. It got so bad that I started sleeping with my money in my pillowcase. When I showered, I would take my cash in the bathroom with me and hide it in a towel under the toilet. I knew I couldn't let my guard down for a second, because if I did, all of my money would be gone. Each day, I felt worse and worse about my living conditions, and I really wanted to move out. Unfortunately, I had nowhere to go. I was having a hard time sleeping at night, and I just knew something bad was going to happen.... and of course it did.

It was mid-afternoon on a beautiful Tuesday in the middle of February, and I was sitting on my couch watching my favorite show on ESPN. The show was almost over, and as soon as it ended, I planned on meeting Justin for lunch. With maybe five minutes left in the show, I thought I heard a soft knock on the front door. I was super lazy, so I didn't really want to get up and check. I assumed if somebody was there, it was one of our friends, so I just yelled, "Come in!" The door opened slowly and a dude poked his head in and said, "Hey man, is Marcus here?" I replied, "Yup," and told him to come on in. A small Mexican man walked in and stood in the doorway. He was maybe 5'7", his neck was covered in tattoos, and he had long, black, slicked-back hair. I had never seen him before, but I just assumed he was there to sell Marcus drugs. He smiled at me and said, "What up."

"What up man!" I replied. "Marcus is back in his room. Just take a right at the hallway, and it's the first door on your left."

There was a long couch by the door, so when he came in I couldn't tell if he was holding anything. But when he turned the corner to walk down the hallway, I noticed what looked like a long, black shotgun case in his left hand. Now, you gotta remember I am from Wyoming, so even though I have never been a hunter, I have seen people carrying guns into other people's houses plenty of times. Granted they usually weren't little Mexican gangsters, but honestly, I didn't think twice about this guy. It was 3 p.m. on a Tuesday, and I lived in the middle of a very busy apartment complex, so in my mind, there was no reason to worry. My only concern was that he didn't shut the front door, which I decided I would do once my show went to commercial. Unfortunately, I never made it to the commercial break.

After being in Marcus's room for maybe two minutes, the little Mexican dude came out of his bedroom, walked into the living room, and was now standing right in front of me. He had a long, black double-barreled shotgun in his hands, and he raised it up and pointed it right at my face. The tip of the gun was about 10 inches from my nose. He said, "Give me all of your money right now." I quickly replied, "Man, I don't have any money." When I said that, he just turned around and started to walk away. I remember thinking, "Is this a joke?" I honestly wasn't scared at all. It didn't feel real. When he walked away, he didn't go back into Marcus's room. Instead, he got to the couch and headed towards the front door. At some point, he must have realized he didn't fully shut it on his way in, so he slammed it shut, obviously aggravated, and locked the deadbolt. When I heard the click it got very real, very fast. Now I knew it wasn't a joke, and I was scared to death. Knowing the door was locked made me feel like I was trapped. After locking the door, he turned around and yelled, "I am not going to tell you again, give me all your fucking money right now!" I had around $4,000 in my pocket, which was all the money I had to my name.

I know what you're thinking. Why in the world would you carry all the money you have? In the gambling business, everything is done in cash. Money is changing hands constantly, so you don't really use banks. If you get a hot tip, you don't have time to go to an ATM or be in and out of the bank all day long. And most gamblers aren't very honest with their winnings on their taxes, so you never really want the government to know how much money you have won. I obviously couldn't hide the money in my room, because my roommate was constantly trying to steal it. So the money always stayed in my front right pocket, where I knew it was safe.

Well, it wasn't safe on this afternoon, and when he asked that second time, I quickly handed him the $4,000 and told him I had a lot more at my bank that was just three blocks away. I didn't have any money at the bank up the street, but he didn't know that. My only thought was that I had to get out of the apartment so I would have some kind of chance to get help. He didn't take the bait on the bank, and told me to stand up. He walked behind me, put the shotgun in the top of my back, and told me to walk to Marcus's room. I walked slowly down the hallway. When I entered the bedroom, Marcus was sitting on the corner of his bed, trying to pretend like he also got robbed. He was trying to act like he was crying, but his bad acting instantly made me realize that I had been set up. I was trying to keep my composure, but on the inside, I was starting to panic. I remember thinking "if I don't get out of this room, I am going to die in this room." I thought about diving head first out the window. We were on the first floor, so, besides the cuts from the glass, I would have landed in a bush and been fine.

Before I could do anything crazy like jump out the window, the Mexican dude said, "Go sit in the corner with your eyes facing the wall, and don't move for 10 minutes. If you move or call the cops when I leave, I will come back and kill you." So, I went and sat in the corner just like he said, just hoping he wouldn't shoot me in the back. I was thinking, "Hey man, you can rob me, but you don't have to put me in time-out like a four-year-old kid." I sat there for what I thought was 10 minutes. Then, I got up and told my roommate, "Fuck you, I know you set me up," and I ran out the front door to my car. The second I got in my car, I started crying. My whole body was shaking, and I knew I had to get the hell out of there. I was having a hard time driving, because I was so upset. I drove two blocks and had to pull over in an Applebee's parking lot. The first thing I did was call Kevin. I told him the whole story and asked him what I should do. He told me to call the police immediately! I argued with Kevin, reminding him that the guy said he was going to come back and kill me if I called the police. Kevin said, "If he was really going to kill you, he would have already done it. Trust me, you need to the call the police." I said, "Okay, I will call you back in a little bit," and I hung up.

I called the police right away. They told me to stay in the parking lot, and they would come meet me there. Five minutes later, two cop cars pulled into the parking lot and had me follow them back to my apartment to give my statement. When we got back to the apartment, Marcus was long gone. While I was telling one of the officers my story, another officer got a call saying they had caught him. The little gangster genius got greedy and must have been feeling confident, because he went and robbed two other houses after he left my apartment. I was relieved, because that meant he was going to jail and couldn't come back to kill me. I was also excited to get my life savings back. I was hungry and really needed a cold beer.

Unfortunately, I didn't know how the justice system worked, and my money was now evidence. It would be months before I would eventually get it back. As soon as the police left, I began to pack up all my stuff. I knew I didn't want to spend another second in that apartment. To this day, I hate that whole complex. I still get an awful feeling in my stomach when I am in Vegas and I drive by those apartments. I don't have one good memory from the time I lived there. Those eight months were a very depressing, dark part of my life. I never saw Marcus again.

That night, I packed up my car with everything I owned and I just drove. I wasn't sure where I was going, I just knew I couldn't go far. I only had a half tank of gas and not a dollar to my name. I completely forgot about my lunch date with my best friend Justin and he called and asked why I stood him up. I told him everything that happened, and without hesitation, he said I could stay on his couch for a while until I got back on my feet. Things were now at an all time low. I was fighting the biggest depression of my life. I had no money, no job, and I was sleeping on my friend's couch. It was also frustrating to know that my dad was somewhere in the world, continuing to ruin my life. I thought I had cut him completely out of my life, but as long as he knew my date of birth, social security number, and my mom's maiden name, he was obviously going to continue to be a problem. I was sad most days, because I really missed Shannon and still thought about her constantly. When I didn't think things could get any worse, I ran into one of Shannon's brothers at the mall. He let me know that she was engaged and was moving to the Pacific Northwest. This crushed me, because we had only been broken up for nine months. It made me sick, knowing that I couldn't sleep at night because I missed her, and she couldn't sleep at night, because she was full of excitement planning her wedding. It just didn't seem fair.

Months later, I found out she got a boob job before the ceremony and married a rich Jewish guy on the 14th hole of a golf course. So much for keeping her body pure and getting married in the temple. I always thought that the only reason Shannon and I didn't make it was because of the Mormon religion, but I guess I just wasn't the right guy. After finding out Shannon was engaged, I spent most days just pouting around Justin's house, being sad. Like so many other times in my life, I once again felt lost, and I didn't know what I was going to do. I thought about moving back home to Wyoming, but there was nothing for me there. I considered going back to college, but then I realized college is expensive and I also suck at going to college. I needed a lucky break, and I needed it fast. And right on cue, I got one.

After taking a long break from playing lunchtime basketball, I decided to return to the gym to try and get some exercise, and to take my mind off of everything that was upsetting me. It was great to see all my friends, and I was shocked how excited they were to see me. I had only been gone a couple months, but they acted like they had seen a ghost when I walked into the gym. After playing three very competitive games, I took a seat under the basket and relaxed. One of the professional gamblers came over and sat down next to me. We spent the next 10 minutes bullshitting about how obnoxious the personal trainers had become. I asked him how the gambling world was going, and he said, "It's funny you asked. Things are going so well that I am looking to put a couple runners out on the strip for football season. Do you have any interest in working for me?" I couldn't say yes fast enough. I was dead broke and I knew the job would not only pay well, but it would also allow me to start getting casino comps again. That meant I could eat, drink, and sleep on the strip for free whenever I wanted. Buffets, free booze, and a king size bed were a dream come true for a guy who was essentially homeless at the time.

I returned to work, and the first day on the job, I quickly realized this was going to be nothing like working for Kevin. My new boss was a 6'8, goofy, Jewish guy that looked like a homeless Howard Stern. His name was Alex Pinkowitz, but everybody just called him Pinky. He was very weird, but also incredibly generous and sweet. He ended up hiring both Justin and me for football season, but he was running a much smaller operation than Kevin and Oliver did. Honestly, it was so small that he didn't even need us. I think he was just paying us to hang out with him, because he didn't have a lot of friends. I was more than happy to get paid to hang out. I was so broke at the time, I would have hung out with my dad for twenty bucks an hour. Okay, well maybe not my dad, but you know what I mean. The best part of working for Pinky was that one of the job requirements was playing basketball before lunch every day. Like Kevin, Pinky always wanted me on his team, because he wanted to win. Now that he was paying me, I would always try to get on his team to make him happy. Unlike Kevin, he was awful at basketball. He was the oldest guy that played with us and was always the worst player on the court. There were a million times I wanted to scream at him for missing a layup or throwing the ball away, but I didn't, because I couldn't afford to get fired. Working for Kevin was so much fun and never really felt like work, where working for Pinky was definitely a job. Pinky knew I had to kiss his ass, and he loved it. Nothing with him was ever easy, because he was very irrational and unpredictable. He literally was always one bad beat away from going crazy. There were countless times he would lose a big bet, and then fall to the floor screaming, "NOOOO!!!!" He would roll around his office screaming and pulling out his own hair like a giant toddler mid-tantrum. Then he would tell us that he was quitting gambling forever, kicking us out of his office. This sucked, because we would become jobless all because some dumb ass 20-year-old kid in Texas missed a field goal.

The good news is, we quickly learned that Pinky was a degenerate and could never actually stop gambling. He would always hire us back two or three weeks later. We would come back to work, and he would act like nothing happened. Over the three years I worked for Pinky, this happened at least seven times. It was a never-ending cycle, and it really sucks when you are living week to week and paycheck to paycheck. After the third time he fired us and then re-hired us, Justin and I decided that we needed to start putting some money away so we would be okay the next time we were fired for no reason. We decided it was time to invent Pinky insurance. At the end of the workday, we returned as usual to Pinky's house in order to turn in our

money, tickets, and casino chips. I started keeping a wad
of money (usually around $4000–$5000) in my front right
pocket, and if I felt like he was busy watching a game or if
it was hectic in the office, I would turn in everything but
that bundle in my front right pocket. This was a free roll
for me, because if he was too busy and let me leave, I had
the money, but if for some reason he did count everything
and said, "Hey Brandt, you're short," I would reply, "Oh
shit, I forgot I had money in this front right pocket. I am
an idiot." and give him the money like it was an honest
mistake. Now, I could only take this free roll once every
three or four weeks, so I had to pick my spots. It worked
the first two times, and Justin and I had a little over $7,000
in our Pinky insurance fund. The third time, he caught it
and said, "You're a fucking idiot, you gotta make sure you
check all of your pockets." The fourth time, we decided
we would let Justin do it. Justin was never in the Mallfia,
so mid-count, he got nervous and gave the money back to
Pinky. Pinky seemed irritated and said, "That's the second
time you dumb fucks have done that; are you guys trying
to steal my money?" We both said, "Of course not, we are
just idiots and forget sometimes." He agreed that we were
idiots, but also seemed suspicious. We decided that day
that we had to retire the "idiot that forgot he had a bunch
of cash in his front pocket plan."

This irresponsible idiot strategy was something
I learned from Kevin, and I perfected over time. On
countless occasions, I watched Kevin play dumb and let

people talk down to him like he was a dumb hick from Ohio. The whole time, he was plotting and calculating how he was going to get what he wanted in the end. He would always tell me, "Let all of these idiots think they are smarter than you. In the end, they will figure out that you outsmarted them... and at that point, it's way too late." This is probably the best advice anybody has ever given me. I still use it every single day of my life. I like to keep expectations very low, and I tell anybody that will listen that I am dumb and useless. Then, while nobody is paying attention to me, I am paying attention to every detail going on around me. There is nothing more rewarding than outsmarting some arrogant asshole that thought he was so much better than you. Eventually, they will figure out that you are very smart and calculating, and then you have to go to another plan. My backup plan is always to be fearless.

Once we knew we couldn't play dumb with Pinky anymore, we just started taking chances. The second installment of Pinky insurance was called "ticket jack." Anytime he went to the bathroom, kitchen, or even left his desk for 30 seconds, we would steal one of his winning tickets. He always kept a big stack of them in the middle of his desk. If we saw an opening, we would snatch a winning ticket from the top of the pile. This became a fun game, because the tickets were worth anywhere from $330 to $4,200. It was like playing a free slot machine that always let us win. We really did love Pinky and didn't want to rob him blind, but we felt like we needed to protect ourselves. We made sure we weren't greedy and tried to only do it once a week. There was no unemployment, and this job would definitely not work as a reference on a resume. We just had to be able to survive when he became irrational and fired us. We built our Pinky insurance up to well over $15,000, and that's what got us through the 4th, 5th, and 6th, times he fired us. When he fired us those times, we were excited, because it meant we got a paid vacation.

Pinky wasn't a bad guy, he just was so fucking weird! To give you an idea of how weird he was, even though he was married, he only loved three things in life: wrestling, punk-rock music, and hamsters. And he loved his hamsters the most. He named one of them Murray, and that name made him sometimes bet thousands of dollars on a small college in Kentucky named Murray State. He didn't care who Murray State was playing, he just had to bet on them because they had the same name as his favorite hamster. Most of the time, Murray State would lose the game, and he would be furious. I always wanted to kill that hamster and get him a brand new one named Duke or Alabama. Why couldn't my job security be based on a hamster named after a college powerhouse?

The absolute worst part of the job was that Pinky started making me hang out with him even when we weren't working. A lot of my weekends consisted of independent wrestling matches in warehouses and teenage punk-rock concerts. He would always say, "If you don't go with me, I can always hire somebody who will." I love going to concerts, but there is nothing worse than being a bored, 27-year old, standing next to a weird 60-year old dude who is rocking out while surrounded by hundreds of teenagers. I must have gone to 25 awful punk band shows during those years, and they all sounded the same. And I hated every single one of them! The wrestling matches were even worse. It was the lowest level of professional wrestling. These matches were full of awful acting and always lasted at least four hours. I would just sit in the audience miserable, dreaming about body slamming Pinky on his stupid face. It really was torture. All of my friends were out having fun, and I had to give up countless Friday and Saturday nights, because I had to keep my boss happy.

This was also the point in my life when I started to really want to try stand-up comedy. I had been dreaming about it ever since Matt had made that mention to me during our lunch in Arizona, and I had finally started to sign up for open mics. To be more specific, I had signed up three times, but then the day of the show, I would chicken out. I remember calling the bar owners or guys that ran the shows and telling all three of them, "Sorry, I can't make it, because my dad died." (Yes, I tried that old trick where you say something happened in hopes that it will actually happen.) My biggest fear wasn't the crowd, it was actually talking into a microphone. I had only done it a handful of times, and every time I did it, my eyes started to water when I heard my voice amplified. I thought, "I can't be the comedian that cries throughout his whole set." I could hear comedy club owners saying, "Oh yeah, the crying comic, that sounds hilarious." At the time, I honestly didn't think I would ever get the courage to go on stage and perform stand-up comedy.

I have always believed that everything happens for a reason, and looking back now, I know meeting and working for Pinky was one of the first steps towards my dream of becoming a comedian. As I said, I hated going to the shitty concerts Pinky would drag me to, but there is one show I will always be grateful to have attended. The lead singer from Pinky's favorite band was playing in LA on a Friday night, and Pinky said we couldn't miss it. He said he wanted me to go, because there was a hilarious comedian opening, and he was sure I would love him. The last thing in the world I wanted to do was drive Pinky all the way to LA. I told him I was really sorry, but I couldn't go. I had never heard of the singer or the comedian, and I knew he was just telling me I would love the show because he wanted me to chauffeur him all the way to LA and back. As much as I fought it, in the end I had no choice. I was going. Pinky was going to pay me to drive. He reminded me again that this was part of my job, and if I didn't like it, I was free to find another job.

We left early on a Friday morning and sat in stop and go traffic all the way to LA. After a miserable six-hour drive, we finally made it to this cool little bar in Hollywood named Largo. We lined up outside of the club, and waited nearly two hours before we got in. Pinky always wanted to sit in the back of the room, so we grabbed a two-top table in the dark back corner. The show started, and it was incredible. The musical act was a guy named Rhett Miller, who is the lead singer of the very successful alternative country band, the Old 97's. At the time, I wasn't familiar with Rhett's music, but I loved every song he played that night. As much as I enjoyed Rhett, the comedian was by far the highlight of my night. He was hilarious! Up to that point, I had only been to live stand-up shows in the comedy clubs in Vegas casinos. The casino shows were always very formal and professional. This comedian was nothing like that. He was wearing a t-shirt, visor, and brought a big notebook with him on stage. What initially impressed me was his demeanor on stage. I couldn't believe how relaxed he was. He would occasionally look at the notebook, but it felt like he was making most of the jokes up on the spot. What I really loved about his set was how much fun it seemed he was having the entire time he was onstage. To this day, I still remember some of the jokes he told that night. He instantly became my favorite comedian, and on that long drive back to Vegas after the show, I made up my mind. I was going to be a comedian!

I performed for the very first time two nights later in the back of a shitty bar called Boomers, which was located just off the strip. I invited all of my friends to the show,

Jamie Sedlmayer 2015

knowing there was no way I could back out if they were all there. I was very nervous before the show started, but I had a couple beers to try to calm my nerves. I was going to be the fifth comic on the show, and I stayed out in the bar alone while the first four comics performed. When the fourth comic was finishing up, the host peeked his head into the bar and said, "You're next." I walked into the back room, and two minutes later they called my name, and I was walking up to the stage. I heard the first big laugh after I finished my second joke, and then the rest of the set is a blur. I did about five minutes total, and it actually went really well. I got a bunch of laughs, my friends all said I was really funny, and best of all, I didn't cry at all during my set. When I walked off the stage that first time, I knew my whole life had changed. I fell in love with stand-up comedy that night, and it became the only thing I thought about.

You are probably wondering who the comedian was that had such an effect on me that night in LA. It was a guy the whole world would fall in love with many years later. Ironically, we actually have something in common. We both broke into Mike Tyson's house... he just did it as the star of one of the funniest comedy movies ever made. It was the hilarious Zach Galifianakis.

After I did that first show, I started hitting up every open mic in town. On the nights I couldn't get on stage, I would hit up one of the five comedy clubs in Vegas. I would get to the showrooms minutes before the shows started, and then slip the door guy twenty bucks to let me sit in the back of the room. I would study the different comics and observe how they worked the crowd. When I couldn't go to a show, I was at home reading comedians biographies and watching comedy DVDs. My newfound comedy obsession left me no time for punk rock concerts and wrestling matches, and eventually Pinky fired me. I was totally okay with being fired, because the stand-up was going great, and I was telling anybody who would listen that I was about to become rich and famous.

What I didn't know at the time is that you really don't make any money during the first 10 years you perform comedy. The first two years, I was performing stand-up about once a week, but was never getting paid in actual cash. I would occasionally get paid with a free drink or appetizer, but at the end of the night, I always had a big

bar tab, so my money was dwindling fast. When Pinky fired me, I had saved up almost $18,000, and I knew that money wouldn't last me forever. But I didn't need it to last forever, I just needed it to get me by until Hollywood discovered me and made me a mega star just like Zach. Unfortunately, Hollywood never came calling, and I quickly realized that to become a great comedian, I had to dedicate my life to the craft.

I had no problem committing my life to it, I just wasn't ready for all of the ups and downs. It really is an emotional roller coaster that takes its toll on your confidence and body. The $18,000 I had saved working for Pinky was dwindling quickly, and I had to go back to living on Justin's couch. When Pinky fired us, Justin got hooked up with a job as a waiter at the hottest sushi restaurant in town. It was a beautiful restaurant called Little Buddha in the brand new Palms Casino. He was making $400 to $500 bucks a night, so being the great friend that he is he didn't charge me rent. He helped me survive, as I was literally becoming a starving artist. At the time, I had no idea how hard the comedy business really was. My funny-new-guy-on-the-scene status quickly wore off, and now I was just another comic who was sitting around complaining about not being able to work in the big comedy clubs. All of my friends had seen me perform a couple of times and had stopped coming to the shows. Most nights, it was just Justin and me in some shitty, smoke-filled dive bar nowhere near the famous Las Vegas strip.

Justin was very instrumental in me chasing my comedy dreams. Not only was he helping me financially, but he was also the one person that believed in me. Those shows were always awful, but he was always there to tell me to kill it right before I went on stage. He was also the first one to tell me I did great every time I came off stage. He really is the best friend everybody should have. He tried to keep my spirits up, which was tough, because, once again, I was broke and I knew I was heading for a serious depression. Most nights I would lie on his couch and stare at the ceiling for hours, questioning every decision I had made in my life that got me to that point. I started drinking a lot, because it was so much easier to sleep when I just passed out. I had no desire to deal with all of the shit that was going on in my head. What drove me crazy was that I knew that I loved comedy more than anything else in my life, but I just wasn't making any money. And, as everybody knows, when you aren't making any money, life gets very hard.

I made the decision that it was time to give up on my dream job and go get a real job. The only thing was, when I tried to get a real job, I was confronted with another

obstacle... my resume. My resume looks a lot like a WNBA box score... it's very unimpressive, and nobody wants to see it. I hadn't held a "on the books" job in nearly nine years, and the two jobs I had held, I had been fired from, both times for being a Mallfia boss. I needed a miracle. By now, we all know that there is only one person in my world that can actually perform miracles, and that's Kevin.

Kevin always came through for me when I needed it the most, but I hadn't expected him to perform any miracles at that point in my life. At that time, he and I were barely even talking. The basketball court that cemented our tight friendship had now made us enemies. This was due to a couple of meaningless pickup games, where we were both stubborn and obviously way too competitive. In hindsight, I really wish I had handled things differently. When I look back, I don't think it really had that much to do with the basketball games. I think it was actually a combination of a couple other things. I had become very jealous that he was in love and spending all of his free time with his girlfriend. We used to spend every day and night together, and now I barely saw him. The best nights of my life had been spent with him, and I simply missed him. I was also sad, because I still missed my ex-girlfriend Shannon and felt so alone. At the time, I just wasn't happy with myself, and I hated the direction my life was going.

The great thing about Kevin was, no matter how much I messed up or disappointed him, or just acted like an arrogant young punk, he was always there for me when

I needed him. Like most great dads are for their sons, I know he isn't my dad, but I will always really wish he and Ron were. Even though I was way too proud to tell him I wasn't doing well, he knew I was struggling, and didn't hesitate to put his own reputation on the line to help me out. There was a new group of professional gamblers in town, and they were looking for some runners. These guys were very young, very smart, and quickly getting very rich. Kevin vouched for me and told them I would be the perfect guy to hire. He told them I had a good relationship with the casinos, I always worked hard, and most importantly their money would always be safe. (He was kind enough to leave out the story about the time my punkass dad stole his $80,000.) His recommendation got me the job, and once again he changed my life.

I was excited to get back to work, and I was determined to save my money this time. The other times I had worked as a runner, I thought that position was the dream job. Now I knew that being a full-time comedian was the job I really wanted. I figured I would work my ass off for a year, and then I would take all the money I had saved up and move to New York City, where I could do multiple shows every single night. When I started the job, I had no idea just how easy it would be to save up so much money. The new guys I was working for were very book smart, but they knew nothing about the streets. This was the first time they had used runners, so they didn't really know how my job was supposed to work. They would send me down to the strip to bet the games, but instead of having me call in the bets the second I made them like Kevin did, or have me bring back the money and tickets each night like Pinky did, they would let me keep the cash and tickets until the next afternoon. I would then turn in the bets I had made the night before when I got to their house around 3 p.m. the next day. They did this, because they were all big boys that loved to go out for fancy meals every night, so the second the betting was done, they wanted to get to dinner. The last thing they wanted to do was wait 45 minutes for me to drive all the way back to their house to turn in the money and the tickets.

This was an absolute jackpot for me. It meant if I bet on the Los Angeles Lakers at five different casinos, for $5,000 a ticket and the Lakers won, I could wake up early the next day, go cash one of the winning tickets, put the $5,000 I bet back in the bankroll like the bet was never made, and I could take the $5000 in winnings for myself! They still won $20,000 on the game, and I won $5,000, so in my mind, everybody was happy. After seven weeks of working for this new group, I went from being dead broke and owing everybody I knew, to paying everybody off and having $37,000 cash under my bed. The whole thing was unreal because it happened so fast.

This is the point where the lessons I learned from my past scams came into play. The way a scam always gets messed up is greed, so I had to fight off greed every night. I was betting so many games, and these guys were so good, there were plenty of nights when I had over 25 winning tickets. I would try to only take $3,000–$5,000 a day, but if they had a big day, I did too! I remember one day they won over $60,000 just with me! And that was with the $14,000 I had already taken out for myself. The job just got better every day. After three months, I was all the way out of debt. Not only did I pay off everybody I owed money, but I also paid off all the debt my piece of shit dad ran up on the credit cards he took out in my name. The bank of Brandt had just over $60,000 dollars cash hidden in an orange Nike shoe box in the wall behind my dresser. Working for these guys was the most lucrative job I had ever had. I was making more money than my lawyer and dentist friends, and the best part was I was only working three to four hours most days.

I was still doing as much stand-up comedy as possible, and I even booked a couple road gigs. Instead of doing five-minute sets, I was now doing 20–35 minute sets, and I began to get a local following. One of my friends started a small comedy management company, and I officially hired her as my manager. Each day, I was getting closer and closer to becoming a professional comedian. Unfortunately, after five months, my manager ended up dropping me because she would book me weekend gigs, and I would never take them. The problem was that they were booking me shows in the Midwest that paid around $600 for six shows. I had dreamed of doing two shows a night in a real comedy club, but these shows were always on Thursday, Friday, and Saturday nights. There was no way I could take these gigs and miss a weekend of work. I was averaging around $3,500 dollars a day on the weekends as a runner. Don't get me wrong, I really wanted to be a stand-up comedian, but my main goal at the time was to never, ever, ever, ever, be broke again.

I had officially fallen into the Vegas trap. I was like every bartender, waiter, and stripper in Las Vegas—I wasn't chasing my dreams and doing what I wanted to do because I was addicted to the fast cash that I could make and take home every night. As time went on, the more knowledgeable my bosses became about the street-side of gambling. They began to make me call in my bets as soon as I made them. They also hired a guy who wouldn't go to dinner with them, but would stay at the house and wait for all the runners to turn in their money and tickets at the end of the night. This really cut into the amount of money I was making each week.

I was still able to make a couple extra-thousand each week on simple math mistakes they would make when they were in a hurry trying to get all the runners out to the streets. They had hired four other runners, so each day around 2:15 p.m., we would all show up to get our bankrolls and that created chaos in the office, because they were trying to bet and get info on the games at the same time. They needed all of the runners on the strip and ready to bet at 3 p.m., so occasionally my bankroll would have more money in it then it was supposed to, and that meant free money for me.

At some point, when they were doing their monthly figures, they realized that there was a lot of money missing. There were five of us working as runners at the time, and they decided they would set us all up to see who came back with the right amount of money and find out who was robbing them. Well, four of us came back with the right amount of money, and one of us was a little short... oops! They had given all five of us $4200 more than they said they had, and I had caught it by the time I gotten to the third casino. The second I knew I was over, I separated $4140 and put it in my right front pocket. Whenever I was taking their money, I wouldn't take their whole mistake, I would just take most of it. If they thought they gave me $92,450, but they really gave me $96,650 I would take $4,140 and put $60 back in the bankroll. That way, when I turned in the bankroll, it would be at $92,510, and they would be happy, because I brought back more money than they thought they sent me out with. They would say, "You are over 60 bucks," and I would say, "One of the dumb sportsbook employees must have given me too much money."

I did that as a way to build their trust. They thought I was super honest by bringing back extra money, when the truth was I secretly taking thousands of dollars from them. Technically, I was working for them, but really I was working for myself. On this day when I returned to the office, I turned in my money and tickets and sat on the floor, nervously waiting for them to tell me I was good to go. Whenever I was over and had extra money stashed in my pocket, I would talk to everybody in the room, trying to humor and distract others in hopes of taking my boss's mind off of counting. The process of counting up all the tickets and cash was long, and if the number wasn't right, it was a pain in the ass to recount it over and over again. I always banked on the fact that my boss was lazy and trusted me.

There were a few times in prior months when my boss came up short on his count, and he just said, "Fuck it, I probably messed up. See you tomorrow." That, unfortunately, was not the case on this day. When my boss finished counting my money for the third time, he made a loud announcement to the room. He didn't even turn around in his chair, he just leaned his head back and said: "It's him." Those two words made the room go silent, and everybody immediately stopped what they were doing. They all looked up from their computers and focused their eyes on me. At that moment, I knew I was in big trouble. The energy in the room completely changed, and the main boss that rarely said much stood up.

"So you're the little cocksucker that has been stealing all of our fucking money!"

I put on my best-confused face, and said, "What are you talking about? I didn't take anything."

"This afternoon, we gave all of the runners too much money, and you are the only piece of shit that didn't bring it all back."

I knew exactly what he was talking about, and I was prepared. I went to my old trick, and said, "Wait... wait... I totally forgot to check this pocket, it's right here. I don't usually use this pocket." It always worked on Pinky so I had no reason to think it wouldn't work on these guys. I had forgotten that these guys were a lot smarter than Pinky, and there were six of them. The head dude looked at me in amazement, and said, "Really? That's quite a coincidence. We have noticed that money is missing, so we set everybody up today, and everybody came back with the right amount... except for you."

I was caught. I had to do something, and I had to do it fast. My heart was pounding so hard, it felt like it was going to pop out of my chest. It felt like I was in the Dillard's conference room all over again. Except this time, when my mobster instincts kicked in, I decided to use a strategy rarely seen in mafia movies... cry, cry, cry. I have seen it work a hundred times for my ex-girlfriends, so I figured I would give it a try. I started crying and saying, "I swear to God, it was an accident. I promise you guys I am not lying." The tears were coming down fast, and I even had snot bubbling out of my nose. I was crying like an 8-year old who was just told he didn't get to trick or treat this year. I begged and pleaded, telling them I needed the job and if they fired me, I didn't know what I would do. I even dug deep and played the "Deadbeat Dad Card." While fake crying as hard as I could, I said, "I don't even have a dad. You guys are the only family I have. Without you guys, I would be dead or homeless on the street somewhere!"

Taking those 60 bucks out of the $4200 that I was over is the only thing that saved me. I told them, "I promise I didn't take your $4200. I swear, I just forgot I had money in my front pocket. If I was going to steal your money, why would I take all of it but 60 bucks?" I got really lucky that the last two bets I made were for $660 and $2200. It made sense that if I had $7000 in my pocket and I made those two bets, I would have $4140 leftover, and I could have easily put that money in my front pocket in a rush. Making those two bets was just a coincidence, but it was an absolute miracle, because it gave my six-person jury a little bit of reasonable doubt. It seemed like the room was divided. I felt like three of them believed me, and three of them didn't. The main boss told me to go home for the night, and I could come back in the morning. He said, "Tomorrow you will either go back to work, or you will be fired, and Greg will drive you around to cash out all of your tickets."

At the time, I had about $30,000 cash under my bed, so financially I would be okay for a while. I also knew if I got fired for stealing, I would never get another job in the gambling business. Like Kevin always said, "Once your reputation is gone in this business, so are you!" I was okay with that. I loved the job when Kevin was my boss, but with him not around, the gambling world had lost its luster. I hadn't talked to Kevin in months, and I was now surrounded by people I would never hang out with if I wasn't gambling. It's just a shady, greedy world, where cash is the only thing anybody is loyal to. When I worked for Kevin, I worked hard for him, because I respected him and wanted him to succeed. When I didn't work for Kevin, I was greedy and just out for the money, just like everybody else.

I had a feeling I was going to be fired the next morning, and all I could think was, fuck it. If I was going out, I was going out with a bang! I drove straight home from work that day and told Justin what happened. He was shocked that they caught me, but not shocked when I told him I needed him to be ready at 8 a.m. the next morning. I decided if they told me I was fired and sent me with Greg to cash out all of my tickets, I would text Justin which casino we were going to first. The second I got to that casino, I was going to get out of the car and make a run for it! Justin would pick me up on the backside of whatever casino we were at, and we would drive around from casino to casino, cashing out all of my tickets as fast as we could. After working the strip for 10 years, I knew every side entrance and back door, so losing Greg would be easy. I'd have no problem outrunning him. He weighed 100 pounds more than me and smoked a pack a day. I also knew I would be running for my life. The house we worked out of was about 25 minutes from the Strip, so I figured by the time they found out I was on the run, I would have a huge head start. I had no doubt Justin and I could get all the tickets cashed before they found us, and our next stop would be the airport. After cashing all the tickets, I would have somewhere around $200,000 in cash, and I would head to my buddy's ranch in Wyoming to hide out for a couple of months.

That night, I didn't sleep a wink. I tossed and turned, thinking about how to get in and out of every casino, and what I would do if my bosses somehow found me before I got to the airport. I headed to work that morning with the plan all set to go. Fortunately for me and everybody else involved, they decided not to fire me. They told me after talking about it for most of the night, they had decided to let me keep my job. I was told from that moment forward, I had better not even make a small mistake, because if I did, I would be fired on the spot. They said they would continue

to set traps to try to catch me, and all of them would be watching my every move! I couldn't believe it. I survived, and I was going back to work. I told myself I would start treating this like a regular job. I would just go to work every day and save every penny. I wanted to get back to focusing on studying or performing stand-up comedy every night of the week. I figured I would work hard for them for maybe eighteen months and then I would move to New York City. I told myself no more side hustles and no more taking chances. It was time do honest work.

The next eight months, I was very proud of myself, because I was on my best behavior. But then, I began to get frustrated and my mentality quickly changed. Everybody working with us started making a lot more money, but my salary continued to stay the exact same. I started spending every day trying to figure out a new plan that would enable me to out-smart the new precautions my bosses had put in place to protect their money. As always, I didn't want to be greedy, but I did want to get what I felt like I deserved. Of course, the way my brain works, I had no problem coming up with a new plan that would allow me to make an extra $3,000–5,000 each week without them knowing. It wasn't as lucrative as the old scam, but it was a lot safer, and the extra money each week was going straight into my move to New York fund.

Some of my friends thought it was fucked up that I was stealing from my bosses, but I justified taking the extra money at work, because I was the one out on the streets literally risking my life carrying that much money. There was no way to be discreet about having that much money, because every time I cashed out anything over $10,000, the casino made a big production of it for the cameras. For example, let's say I cashed out $50,000 in tickets, which I did at least once a day. It would take at least 10 minutes to complete the process, as the ticket writer had to count out every $100 bill. While he was slowly counting, every degenerate, low-life in the sports book watched every hundred-dollar bill hit the counter and then go into my pockets, before I walked out onto the strip. Often, I would see people whispering and pointing, and I had no doubt there were countless conversations about the best way to rob me. I think the only reason nobody ever attempted to rob me on the strip was because I never gave them a chance. I was always very conscious of my surroundings and moved fast and with a purpose. There are so many cameras in and around the casino that a person would have to be crazy to try it there. But, there was no shortage of crazy people in and around the casinos, so I kept my guard up at all time. I felt like the only way to actually get me would be to follow me home and rob me. If you tried that, though, you had competition, because my father and roommate had the exact same plan.

The other way I justified taking my extra cut was because I was the one doing all the hard work. I was running up and down the strip in 100-degree heat, while they barked orders at me from their air-conditioned mansion. When I got back to the mansion, my bosses were always talking about what exotic island they would visit, and which expensive car they should buy next. I spent every day watching my bosses and the casinos make a ton of money, so I wasn't going to be the only one not getting rich! I was a one-man army, and every day I told myself it was me against everybody in Vegas. I ran my new scam all the way through the end of basketball season, and it was very successful. I was able to save up another $40,000 without anybody in the office suspecting a thing.

The gambling world was like going to high school. You worked for nine months and then it was summer break. The only thing going on in June and July was baseball, and we always got destroyed when we tried to bet baseball, so we would just take the summers off. I was excited when we quit working, because it gave me a lot of free time to do comedy shows and travel the country with my girlfriend at the time, Alex. That summer was easily the best summer of my life. My girlfriend was very rich, and I had all the money I saved for my big move to New York burning a hole in my pocket. We plowed through most of my money and a ton of hers doing everything we had ever dreamed about. We spent around $60,000 in just over two months. We liked to wake up, pick something we have always wanted to do, and then go do it. That led us to Chicago for our first time at Wrigley Field, and Nashville to see the legendary James Taylor, then off to Barcelona, Spain to see a soccer game, with a quick stop in Paris for a few romantic nights. We were like Make a Wish kids, but, lucky for us, we weren't sick, we were just rich.

Now, I know what you are thinking. After everything I have been through and all of my financial up and downs, why would I be blow all of the money I saved? That was the money I set aside for the sole purpose of moving to New York City and chasing my comedy dreams. Of course, I should have used that money to get myself to New York City. Except, now there was a new plan. I had overheard my bosses talking about a new computer program projected to make them a lot of money the following football season. That excited me, because I knew if they were going to make a bunch of money, then I was going to do the exact same thing. The sad thing was, I had a place to live in New York City and everything was set up for me to hit the ground running. I should have been on the first flight out of Vegas the day we quit working, but there was one thing stopping me. The same thing that ruins most people's Vegas experience... GREED! I figured, why move with $20,000 when I could wait six months and go with $200,000?

So, after blowing most of my money that summer, I was down to my last $8,000 with two weeks of break left until preseason football started. It was time to get back to work, and I was counting down the days. There was so much excitement around the office, because everybody wanted to see how the new million-dollar program would work. Unfortunately, I will never know how the program worked, because I didn't make it to football season. After living in Vegas for over ten years, I thought I had seen

it all. I could have never dreamed up what was about to happen next.

My bosses were nice guys, but if I am being honest, they were computer nerds. They were fun, genuine, sweet, had plenty of money to take girls out, but they just didn't have any game. I had tried to introduce them to some of the girls I was friends with, but my female friends weren't interested in them. Instead, my bosses, being great with computers, came up with a romantic computer strategy. Earlier that year, they started video-chatting with girls in Thailand. At first, it was just once or twice a week, but over time, they started to love the attention these girls were giving them. After a couple months, it became a nightly tradition to get online after all the games ended, and talk to these young girls for a few hours. They were teaching the girls English, and at the same time, falling in love with their students. After months and months of chatting online, they decided it was time to take a flight overseas to meet their new ladies. I was excited for them, because they were great guys who just wanted to be in love.

I was going to watch the house while they were gone, but two days before they were supposed to leave, I got a call saying not to worry about it. At the last minute, Greg had decided he didn't want to go on the trip. He would take care of the house while they were gone. Unfortunately, something happened one of the nights when Greg was staying at the house by himself, and he freaked out. He started melting down and kept calling his mom, who lived in Phoenix. She was trying to calm him down and assure him that everything would be okay, but at the end of their last phone call, Greg just hung up. His mom was worried sick about him and didn't know what to do. She couldn't sleep that night, and she repeatedly tried to call him back, but he didn't answer. The next morning, she drove from Phoenix to Vegas to check on her son. Greg had a bad back and was diagnosed bipolar, so he was taking a couple of different medications. Despite that he was always a very relaxed, happy person, so this behavior was very out of character. When Greg's mom arrived to our work house in Las Vegas, she rang the doorbell over and over and got no response. She started to panic. She didn't know what to do, so she called the police. The police came to the house. When their pounding on the front door resulted in no response, they decided to jump the back wall to see if they could look in the back windows. When they jumped over the wall, the first thing they saw was a dead body floating in the pool. It was Greg. He had taken his own life.

The police, went inside and searched the entire house. They were very intrigued by the gambling setup in the basement. Nobody in Vegas has a basement, mainly because it is so hard to dig through the sedimentary rock, so I would imagine the second they saw the staircase leading underground, they thought we were up to something. When they went downstairs, they saw a huge room full of flat screen TV's, computers, money counting machines, and sports betting notes all over the desks. The police assumed we were bookies and confiscated everything. We had three safes hidden throughout the house and they found all three of them. When it was all said and done, the police had taken around $2.3 million dollars in cash, casino chips, and winning sports betting tickets.

Days later, my bosses came home from Thailand and took a limo from the airport to their house. They were happy to be home, and feeling better than ever after having a great week of vacation. When they pulled up, they saw Greg's car was in the driveway and the front door was wide open. They thought it was a little weird that the door was open, but just assumed Greg had run back inside to grab something. They grabbed their luggage and walked up the driveway to the front door. The second they stepped foot in the house, they knew something bad had happened. The entire house was a mess, and they immediately noticed that the safe hidden in the floor of the front room was gone. They called for Greg over and over and searched every room looking for him, but he was nowhere to be found. Once they saw that all the money was gone, they realized they had been robbed and started to worry that something bad might have happened to Greg. They called the police and told them, "We have been robbed, and we think our friend has been kidnapped!" The police said, "We hate to tell you this, but your friend is dead, and we have all of your stuff. You can come see us at your earliest convenience, and we strongly suggest you bring your lawyers with you."

I had no idea anything happened at the house, and I was shocked when I got a phone call early the next morning from my boss. I answered the phone and said, "What's up buddy, how was your trip?" My boss replied, "I got bad news. Greg is dead." I was shocked and asked what happened. He didn't go into any details, he just replied, "Just so you know, we are moving to Costa Rica tomorrow." I said, "What do you mean you're moving tomorrow? What about football season?" He told me the police in Vegas now thought we were doing something illegal, so their lawyers advised them to start working from Costa Rica until all of this blew over. Since the gambling world is a cash business, let's just say some people's tax reports may not always be exactly accurate. I was stunned and said, "Well, what about me?" He said, "It's over." Starting to panic, I said, "What do you mean, it's over?" He calmly said, "It's all over."

I was so confused and had so many questions. I started to ask my first question, but the only answer I got was the sound of the dial tone. He had already hung up. They moved to Costa Rica the next day, and I never saw or heard from them again. It really was over, and it all happened in the blink of an eye. I knew that phone call was officially the end of my life as a runner on the Las Vegas strip. Even if I wanted to get back into the gambling business, I don't think I would have been able to. All of the sports betting had moved off-shore with the 24-hour convenience of online betting. So the runner job had pretty much become extinct. The local Vegas casinos had become so corporate that there really wasn't much value in having runners on the streets. And honestly, the gambling life had kind of lost all of its luster. Greg had just passed away, and it made me sad that a friend's death couldn't even get these guys to take a day off. As much as I enjoyed always having a pocket full of cash, I wasn't happy in Las Vegas. All I thought about was being a stand-up comedian. I wanted to be on a different stage performing every single night. I thought about moving to Phoenix where my brother was living happily with his two adorable dogs, just minutes from my mom's house. But at the time the Phoenix comedy scene was dead. I knew to be a great comedian, I needed to head for one of the coasts. My heart and mind said get out of Vegas, which was not going to be easy, considering I had spent the last couple of months plowing through all of the cash I had saved up for the big move. I told myself, go anywhere, just leave town as soon as possible. Even though Las Vegas had changed my life and given me opportunities I never dreamed, in the end, I hated every single inch of that neon-light, slot-machine-ringing, shit hole of a town.

Looking back on my 11 year Vegas experience, I realized I made it longer than most, but in the end, I never had a chance. I was far from an exception to the rule. Sin City was going to beat me, just like it beats everybody else. Of course, it took all of my money. It eventually does that to everybody, but it got me much worse than most dumb tourists. It gave me, and then took away, all of the most important people in my life. I went there with the dream of rekindling a relationship with David and finally having a dad. Vegas let me have that dream for a little bit, but then crushed it. I was left with not even a shadow of a doubt that I will NEVER see him or speak to him again. I fell in love with a beautiful, amazing, blonde girl, who I thought I was going to spend the rest of my life with. Then, one day I woke up, and she was gone forever.

The one that hurt the most was Kevin. Vegas gave me a hero in Kevin, and then took him too. He was the world's best boss and the person I looked up to most. As a kid, I wanted to be Michael Jordan or John Elway, but as an adult, I wanted to be Kevin. In my eyes he was perfect, and I spent every day studying his every move. At the beginning of our friendship, I always loved watching the way his kids looked at him in admiration and complete amazement. It wasn't long until I realized I was looking at him the exact same way. He was my role model, mentor, and most importantly, my best friend. He was the first person in my life I completely trusted and was my first phone call if I needed anything in the world. He taught me about character, responsibility, leadership, generosity, and how to be a man. Kevin also showed me how to be THE man. I learned how to charm people and take over a room the second I walked in. I have met a lot of people who have a ton of friends and are very popular, but I have never met a person that everybody in their life just never wanted to disappoint them. To this day, I don't go a day without thinking about everything he taught

me and how much fun we had.

All of the people I really loved in Vegas were no longer a part of my life, and it was time for me to go, too. There was no way I could afford to move to New York, Luckily, I had a few comedian friends who lived in Los Angeles offer me a free couch for a couple months. That made my decision very easy. My new home would be in beautiful California. I packed up everything I owned in two old, black suitcases and took a cab to the bus station. I was the first person to board the bus, and I took the window seat in the very last row. I watched the bus fill up with maybe 35 people, who all looked like they also just had their dreams crushed. As we pulled out of town, I stared at the dirty bus floor and with tears rolling down my face, I said loudly, "FUCK YOU, LAS VEGAS." Everybody on the bus burst into laughter, and the little hesitation I had to leave Vegas— and that lifestyle—was instantly gone. I was going to Los Angeles to be a professional comedian and make the whole world laugh.

ANXIOUSLY WAITING FOR

The End

Previous Page:
A Nirvana Maze has no discernible entry point. There is a path to get to the exit from anywhere inside the maze. To play the Nirvana Maze game, pick any starting point anywhere inside the maze (whose walls represent Samsara). There is a path to get to the exit from anywhere inside the maze. (Both, the path and all of the reality outside the walls, represent Nirvana.) Your goal is to find that path. If you hit a blind alley, just turn around and try a different path. Try remembering the blind alleys you had hit before, so you can avoid repeating the same mistakes again and again. Note that I am not providing an official solution to this maze. That is because there are as many solutions as there are the possible starting points which you need to pick yourself. And since only you know where you are at any given moment, only you can find the path that leads out of Samsara to Nirvana.

By AdamStanislav, OpenClipArt

You are probably wondering what happened to my dad. Well, your guess is as good as mine. I know he is still alive, but I have never seen or heard from him since our failed game of garage putt-putt with his internal organs. Luckily, we have had no communication, and if it's up to me, we never will. Truthfully, I really hope my dad dies tomorrow. I know that is a strong statement, and if you have a great relationship with your dad I am sure you are thinking, "Wow that's really aggressive." I think most people feel that, no matter what a father has done, you should never wish for him to die. But I disagree.

Now, I would never wish death on your dad, because your dad is probably a great guy. I hope your dad lives to be 241 years old, but after reading this book, you now know how bad my dad is consistently. So, I hope you understand why I hope he doesn't make it to 2:41 p.m. tomorrow. I just don't want him in my life, and I definitely don't need him. For a long time, there was a big part of me that wanted him around, but I hope he knows at no time did I ever need him.

He missed most of my birthday parties, but that was okay, because my aunt and cousins were always there with a table full of presents, an ice cream cake full of candles, and tons of hugs and kisses. He wasn't at my basketball games, but that was okay because my coaches and teammates were always there with a high-five, telling me how proud of me they were. He wasn't at my graduations, but that was okay, because my girlfriend was always right there when I got off stage to give me a big kiss, a hug, and to scream "YOU DID IT!" (She even drove 75 miles to be there for my fake college graduation). He wasn't there to teach me how to become a man, but that was okay, because my step dad was there to show me how to change a tire, shave my face, light a grill, and most importantly, to treat everybody with respect and be a gentleman. He wasn't there on my bad days, but that was okay, because my friends were always there to go for a walk, bike ride, or just sit on my front porch and listen to me complain. They always let me know that I was going to be fine without him. He wasn't there every day, but that was okay, because my mom and grandparents were there every day, all day, no matter what! My brother and I always had everything we ever wanted and needed. My grandparents and mom were all we ever needed.

When people hear my story, sometimes they feel sorry for me, but all of the ups and downs are the best thing that ever happened to me! When I moved to LA, I was just another 6-foot white guy in a town full of better looking 6-foot white guys. But what has separated me from all those other generic white guys is my journey. All the stuff that people thought would ruin my life is actually what has made it possible for me to live beyond my wildest dreams. I literally have out dreamed my own dreams. Every day, I am doing my dream job, and best of all, I live in Hollywood as a stand up comedian! I will save all my comedian stories, for another day, and the next book. But suffice to say, this job has afforded me so many opportunities to do things that I never dreamed were possible. I will say it again, because I am constantly reminding myself... I out dreamed my dreams! All my life, I have heard clichés like, "What doesn't kill you makes you stronger" and, "You

are confined only by the walls you build yourself," but, in my opinion, you don't need any of that. All you really need is these two words... Keep Going! I never imagined I would have this life, and if you asked me to retrace the steps to tell you how I got here, I couldn't do it. All I know is, through all the ups and downs and laughs and tears, I always told myself, "KEEP GOING!" I still find myself constantly repeating those two words. Sometimes I just think it in my head, other times I write them down on a bar napkin, and when I am really struggling, I step outside and scream them as loud as I can. Anytime I think,

see, or hear, those two words, it refocuses me and gets me right back on track. I hope this book inspires you to keep going in every aspect of your life. Believe in your journey, it's what separates you from everybody else. One day I hope I get to meet you after one of my stand-up shows. One day hopefully you can tell me that you have taken a Free Roll and out-dreamed all of your dreams. And one day, hopefully I can tell you that my piece of shit, Free Roll for Disaster dad is finally dead.

Acknowledgements

We did it! We wrote a book! And I say "we" because there is no way I could have done this alone. I thanked over 4000 people in my original acknowledgement, but my editors told me I had to cut it way down. So if you have been a part of my life at all in the last 39 years, I thank you. Everybody that has come in and out of my life has shaped me and helped me become the man I am today.

The first person I have to thank is Keith Sexton; you changed my whole life. I have no idea where I would be at if I would have never met you. You taught me how to be a businessman, a father, and a great friend. You will always be the most important person to ever come into my life and you will always be my hero. Not a day goes by where I don't think about you and laugh, or ask myself what you would do in the situation. Thank you Tracy, Paul, Nate, and Matt for inviting me into your home and treating me like the one thing I really wanted to be... a Sexton. I will never forget the hundreds of amazing nights we shared in the Fountains.

My Best Friends

Justin Dupree you are my best friend and I will be there for you anytime anywhere. You have never once let me down and everybody deserves a best friend like you. Andrew Sleighter, all I want to know is, "What's for lunch?" I look forward to figuring that out with you well into our 90's. Your friendship has made me a better person, and I thank you! To my little bro, Shane Redman, I am so proud of the man you have become. I always knew you would be great and I look forward to spending hundreds of nights with you and your beautiful family over the next 50 years. Love ya Candice and Reign! Through it all I have been so lucky to have my Wyoming/Vegas crew of Vickie, Jill, and Derek with me every step of the way. The four of us know way too much about each other. We have had decades of fun together, and I promise to get rid of all of the embarrassing

pictures I have of you guys if you do the same. Things have just gotten better when you guys added Chris, Clint, Sophia, Mason, Reed, and Paxson. Without the Girany and Scearce families, I would have never been in L.A. chasing my dreams.

You guys have been so supportive of everything I have done, since day one, and I love you guys more then you know. Thank you Ryan Kreppein for taking a shot and being my charming, handsome, relentless manager. Sometimes I think you care about my career more than I do, and I love that. You started as a great friend and now you are my fearless leader who I would follow anywhere. I promise one day your belief in me will pay off handsomely. I am nothing without my future groomsmen. (though who knows when this wedding will happen?) This is my core group of friends that are all guys that I have always looked up to and inspired to be like since the day I met them. They are all family men who are loyal, hilarious, hard working, high character guys that have been there with me through all my ups and downs. Brandon "gooch' Hahn, Brian Moote, Chance Snell, Colin Hardy, Jonath Jackson, Matt Markman, Randy Philbin, Richard Valdez, Ryan Schaffer, and Steve Kisicki… keep your passport updated, because I WILL be getting married in Costa Rica sometime in the next decade.

My Support System

The next group of people are very close friends that have given me a piece of their lives. We have drank way too much, ate all of the BBQ, taken road trips, shared meals, laughed, cried, and dreamed together. They gave me rides to the airport, went skinny dipping with me, shot hoops, snuck into concerts, screamed at TV's during our favorite sporting events, borrowed each others'clothes and never returned them, and made so many incredible memories that I will never forget.

These people have been and hopefully will continue to be a part of my journey:

Andy Burge
Andy and Erin Pannell
Aaron Hansen
Aaron Ontiveroz
Adam, Caroline and
   Zayden Swanton
Ali and Scottie Godino
Andrew and Casey Nath
Andrew Joannides
Anthony Ortiz
Anthony Thurston
Barry Stoss
BS Williams
Ben and Matt Vines

Wild Bill, Lisa, Katie, and
   Scott Brenske
Keyon "Booya" Vanover
Bri and Cash Stephens
Britt Bath
Brandon Muller
Brian and Emily Longbottom
Bryan Bruner
Bryan, Sara, Brock, Dane,
   and Ea Pedersen
Carmine Amonica
Casey Daugherty
Casey and Carrie Schmidt
Cathy and Lincoln Markman

Chad Delura
Chad and Tawny Denick
Chris, Khalilah, and
    Myles Alan
Colman, Rachael, and
    Quinn Lechner
Devin O'Neal
Danielle Booth
Damien and Dylan Verley
Dave and Shelia Bush
Dave Osterberg
Del Jimenez
Dennis, Cindi, and
    Mindi Tobler
Diaz Mackie
Dr. Hector and Maria
    Rodriguez-Luna
Eddie Jayy Conover
Eric, Samantha, and
    Pat Jacobsen
Eric and Ricky Reid
Ericka Smith
Fran Hite
Franco Garcia
Garrett Plumber
Glen, Vicki, Brandi and
    Levi Woolington
Greg and Chris Asay
Greg and Sierra Fulton
Heather Snow
Heidi Hayward

Holly Martinez
Honour Hook
Jackie Robbins
Jamie "Maddog" Mattern
Jared and Kristen Morrow
Jason Bott
Jay Larson
Jed Moore
Jeff Dye
Jenna Green
Jenni and Nikki Dennison
Jenny Tiedeken
Jeremy and Gavin Monjaras
Jeremy Ward
Jill Kimmel
Joe Milczewski
John Hilder
John W, Amy, and
    Duke Klinker
John Roedel
Jon Judy
Josh Cheney
Josh Nasar
Josh Nelson
Julie Seabaugh
Justin Downing
Katharine Sherrer
Kelsey Good
Kevin and Holly Olson
Kevin, Kathy, Shelton,
    and Colby Keller

Krissy and Jose Barragan
Kristin Mackey
Kyle and Jeni Schrawyer
Lance Patrick
Laramie Wassertoff
Lauren and Katie Blaser
Leanna Thomas
Macradee Aegerter
Margo Mccleery
Matt and Beth Farwell
Matt Stephan
Michael and Cori Schrinar
Micheal and Piper Rauzi
Michelle and Mark Guyot
Mike and Crystal
    Cummings
Michael Turner
Mitch Burrow
Myra, Marcus, and
    Matthew Morris
Nathan Lund
Nick and Lisa Meeker
Pat and Kilian Moote
Paul Ames
Paul Taylor
Riley Gallu
Rob Val Adriana and
    HUGO Etchepare
Ryan and Nicole Cameron
Ryan, Jessica and
    Morgan Dickson

Ryan Mutschelknaus
Ryan Rodekohr
Ryan Seals
Ryan Sickler
Rusty and Maria Kunkle
Sarah and Jerimiah Beeken
Sarah Sutter
Shae Buettner
Shane Smith
Shuli Egar
Steph Alex and Danielle
    Kirby
Steph Puleio
Stevenson Brooks
Tagg Lain
Tamaran Conover
Taylor Haynes
Terri Trautwein
Thia Mullikin
Tim Price
Tim and Suzi Schmidt
Tim and Patty Walsh
Todd Smith
Todd Tucker
Tommy, Paula, Christian,
    and Shelby Osborne
Trey Stephens
Wendy Williams
Whitney Sturman
Will LeDoux
Zach and Erin Casey

Mi Casa Su Casa

It didn't matter if I was thousands of miles from home or just down the street, these families all treated me like one of their own. A lot of nights I was just in town to do a show and they were always there with home cooked meals, spare bedrooms, couches, air mattresses, cold beers, tequila shots, birthday cakes, washers and dryers, holiday leftovers and what I need the most - hugs and love.

Brenske	Haynes	Markman	Simon
Costantino	Jacksons	Medina	Sleighter
Creech	Jacobsens	Moote	Taylor
Denisson	Johnsons	Osborne	Valdez
Godino	Kisicki	Pedersen	Walsh
Graham	Lamborn	Redman	
Grant	Lebatard	Rodekohrs	
Hardy	Lewis	Sextons	

The Vegas gambling crew led by the big O and the big brother I always wanted, Tony Enard! Thank you Otis, Dinky, Big Matt and your crew. Thank you Scottie Pritchard, Jamie Shea, Julia "Goolia"Durham, B Woods, and Lex for teaching me about seven team parlays, strippers, hookers, buffets, royal flushes, comps, incredible sex, fine dining, and surviving that awful feeling of walking into a bar in the dead of night and then hours later walking out into daylight.

There are over a hundred comics that I could thank individually, but you all know how lazy I am, so I am just going to keep it short and sweet... THANK YOU to all the comics for letting me be a part of the coolest fraternity in the world. I love almost all of you! There are so many talented men and women in this world giving up everything they have to chase their comedy dreams. Please go out to a show and support them anytime you get the chance.

Thank you Surf Wyoming for always keeping me looking fresh, Don Carlos Taco Shop for always keeping me full, and LA Comedy Club, Brad Garrett's Comedy Club and all of the Funny Bones across the country for continuing to let me grace your stages!

Thank you Jennifer Furioli and Nikki Ward for being great friends who were so generous with your time and talents helping your broke friend make a book! I can't thank you two enough. Without your help this would just be a .pdf on a stolen computer somewhere in Mexico.

Thank you Brad Garrett for making this whole thing happen. You saying, "just give

Charissa Feathers Photography

me 30 pages" made this book come to fruition. They say you never want to meet your heroes, but I am calling bullshit on that one. Brad is one of the most generous and genuine guys I have ever met. Meeting him has brought nothing but great things into my life. I hope the excitement I feel every time his name pops up on my phone never goes away… "HOLY SHIT BRAD GARRETT JUST TEXTED ME AGAIN."

Most importantly I want to thank my family.

Thank you Aunt Talla for being so supportive, sweet, and keeping me in clean underwear every Christmas and birthday.

Thank you Trenton for being my Cheyenne partner in crime who always has a cold beer, home-cooked meal, warm bed, and night of fun planned for me when I come to town. I am so proud of you for becoming a great teacher, coach, and friend!

Killa Kado, you are the funniest and most loyal guy in my life. If I only had one phone call in the world, I am calling you. I know you would do anything and everything for this family and NOBODY gets shit done like you do.

My step dad Ron who stepped in and raised two little punk boys when he didn't have to. Growing up he was a great teacher, coach, mentor, and friend. He is still a very huge part of my life and my fellow road dog.

My little brother and sister Ryan and Hayley, who are two of the sweetest people in the world. They have always supported all of my awful decisions and the second I see either one of them I am instantly happy. I love you both so much, and know Big Bro is here anytime you need me.

My mom, who is the toughest person I know. She is a fighter, a survivor, and my favorite person in the world. She gave us everything we needed growing up and I know she will be there anytime I need her. I love you so much mom and I promise I will give you some grandkids soon.

And finally, thank you Grandma and Grandpa Petty for everything you did for our family. I am sure you are enjoying watching every second of this crazy ride I am living, and I just wish you were here to be a part of it. I miss you guys everyday!

CPSIA information can be obtained
at www.ICGtesting.com
Printed in the USA
LVHW03s2210060818
586124LV00015B/945/P